# Port Hope Ontario Book 4 in Colour Photos, Saving Our History One Photo at a Time

Photography
by Barbara Raué
©2019

Series Name: Cruising Ontario

Book 233: Port Hope Book 4

Cover photo: 57-59 King Street, Page 5

# Series Name: Cruising Ontario
## Saving Our History One Photo at a Time
### in colour photos

Books Available in Alphabetical Order:
Aberfoyle, Acton, Ajax, Alton, Amherstburg, Ancaster, Arthur, Auburn, Aylmer, Ayr, Beaver Valley, Belgrave, Belleville, Bloomingdale, Blyth, Brantford, Brockville, Burford, Burlington, Caledon, Caledonia, Cambridge, Carlow, Chatsworth, Clifford, Collingwood, Conestogo, Delhi, Dorchester to Aylmer, Drayton, Drumbo, Dundas, Dunlop, Eden Mills, Elmira, Elora, Erin, Essex, Fergus, Goderich, Grimsby, Guelph, Hagersville, Hamilton, Hanover, Harriston, Hespeler, Jarvis, Kingston, Kingsville, Kitchener, Lake Superior, Lincoln, Linwood, Listowel, London, Lucknow, Merrickville, Mono, Mount Forest, Mount Pleasant, Neustadt, New Hamburg, Newboro, Newport, Niagara-on-the-Lake, Niagara Falls, North Bay, Oakville, Onondaga, Orangeville, Orillia, Oshawa, Owen Sound, Palmerston, Paris, Pelham, Perth, Peterborough, Petrolia, Pickering, Port Colborne, Port Elgin, Portland, Preston, Rockwood, Sarnia, Sault Ste. Marie, Seaforth, Sheffield, Shelburne, Simcoe, Smiths Falls, Smithville, Southampton, St. Catharines, St. George, St. Jacobs, St. Marys, St. Thomas, Stoney Creek, Stratford, Thamesford, Thunder Bay, Tillsonburg, Toronto, Waterdown, Waterford, Waterloo, Welland, Wellesley, West Flamborough, Westport, Whitby, Windsor, Wingham, Woodstock

Book 218-219: Uxbridge
Book 220: Port Perry
Book 221-222: Stouffville
Book 223: Colborne
Book 224: Bolton/Grafton
Book 225-229: Cobourg

Book 230-233: Port Hope

# Table of Contents

Port Hope is located in Southern Ontario about 109 kilometers (68 miles) east of Toronto and about 159 kilometers (99 miles) west of Kingston. It is located at the mouth of the Ganaraska River on the north shore of Lake Ontario, in the west end of Northumberland County. Port Hope's nearest urban neighbor (25 kilometers to the west) is the City of Oshawa.

Before there were sidewalks, before there were buildings and even before the native Canadian people began visiting Pemedash Wationg (Fat Fire Creek) or Cochingomink, the salmon found a natural home in Port Hope. The salmon ran in huge schools up the Ganaraska River and attracted native Canadians to the harbor.

The first recorded white visitor was a Sulpican monk around 1670, but many European traders called at Ganaraska during the seventeenth and eighteenth centuries. The potential for trade with the Indian population attracted our first builder, Peter Smith who set up a fur trading postherein1788.

Land grants and United Empire settlers soon followed and by 1798 the land grants were secure and forty families were settled. A grist mill and a lumber mill soon followed and Hope Township's port was established in the valley at the mouth of the Ganaraska River.

The town grew rapidly from four families of English descent who arrived by boat in 1793 and settled at the river mouth. Until then the area had been home to aboriginal groups — Huron, then Iroquois, and finally Mississauga — attracted by the salmon and sturgeon that swarmed in its river. More families arrived including blacksmiths, carpenters, bricklayers, and merchants. The mills drew farmers from fifty and sixty kilometers away.

In 1856 the Grand Trunk Railway connected Port Hope to Toronto and the Atlantic seaboard. Its viaduct over the Ganaraska River was the second greatest engineering challenge on the route, exceeded only by bridging the St. Lawrence River at Montreal.

Another railway heading north from Port Hope opened up the vast timberlands and new farms of central Ontario and stretched to Peterborough and Lindsay. Eventually it reached Georgian Bay, at Midland. Down this line came great loads of timber and grain. Some went east to England, but most was exported to the USA through Rochester across the lake.

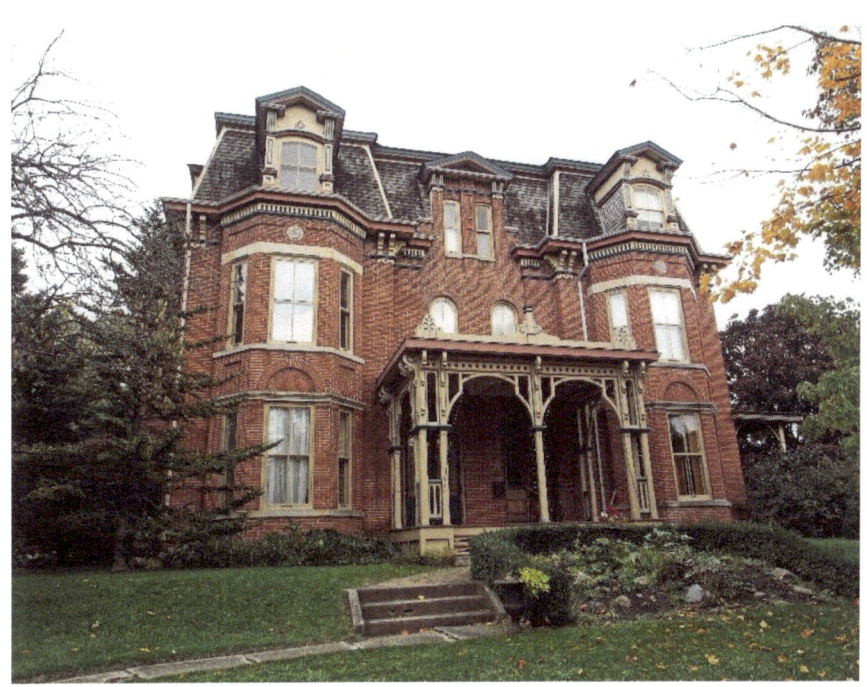

57-59 King Street - Charles Clemes Duplex - c. 1876 -
This semi-detached brick house is in the Second Empire style.
Its colossal three-storey scale is more impressive because of
the semi-detached arrangement, symmetrically divided. Both
halves of the composition contain a complex array of detail.
The distinguishing elements are the steeply pitched mansard
roof in cedar-shingles, and the gabled dormers with eaves
returns and moulded pilasters framed around segmentally-
arched windows. A third facade dormer, centrally placed,
boasts slender lights and is topped with a bracketed pediment.

The facade has two-storey bay windows trimmed with
band courses and decorative panels in brick; dentilled cornice
and paired brackets; slender windows with original glazing
intact, some flat arched, some with segmental arches, some
round headed; twin entrances with prominent arched
transoms and panelled double doors.

Charles Clemes (1814-1878) was a dry good merchant with a store at the corner of Ontario and Walton Street that offered "groceries, provisions, crockery glass, and painted ware." He was originally from Bodmin, Cornwall, England, and came to Canada in 1856 with his wife Ann and their children, Charles Pascoe, John Pope, Kate, Matthew, Charlotte Ann and William Peter. His wife Ann died in 1858. Charles married Phoebe Lonsdale (1833-1890) and had a second family of six children, two of whom died as babies. Family members of his first family resided in one half of the Clemes Duplex, while Charles and his second wife and family resided in the other half.

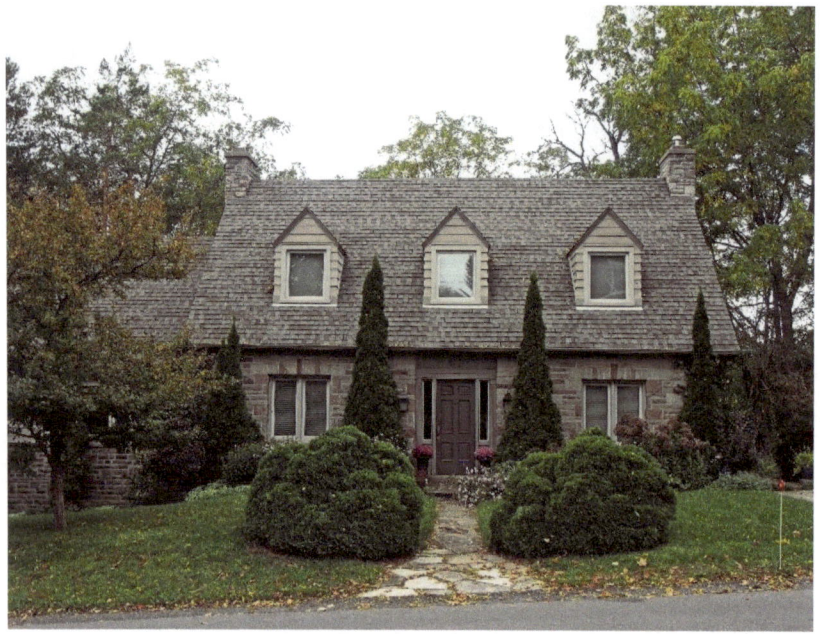

King Street - dormers

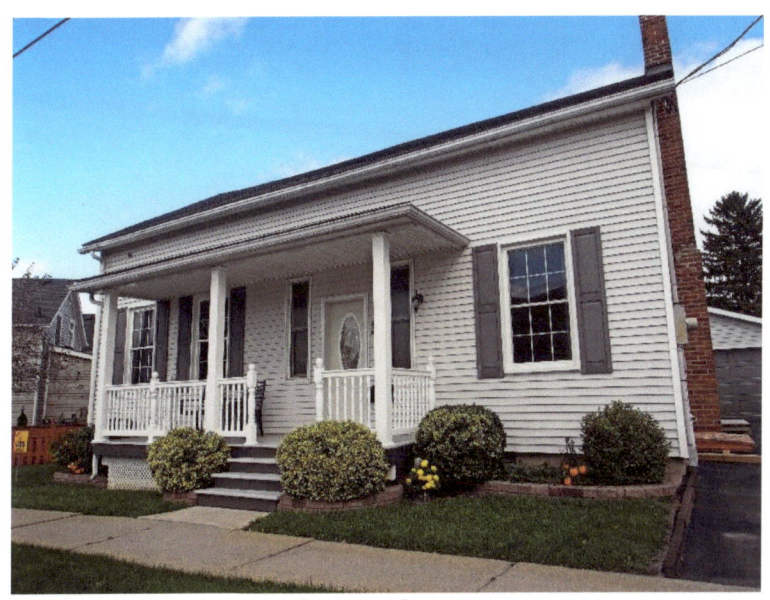

3 King Street

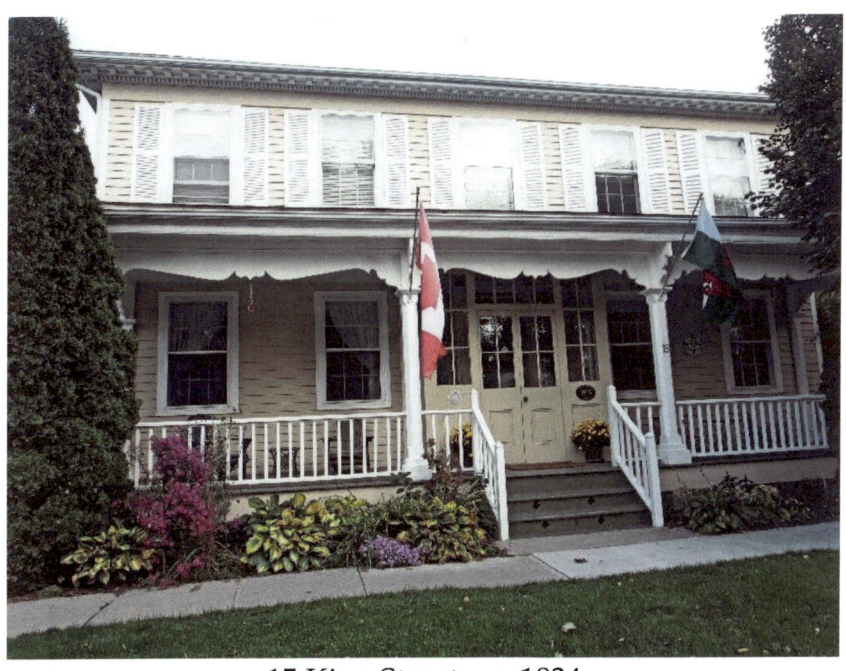

15 King Street – c. 1834

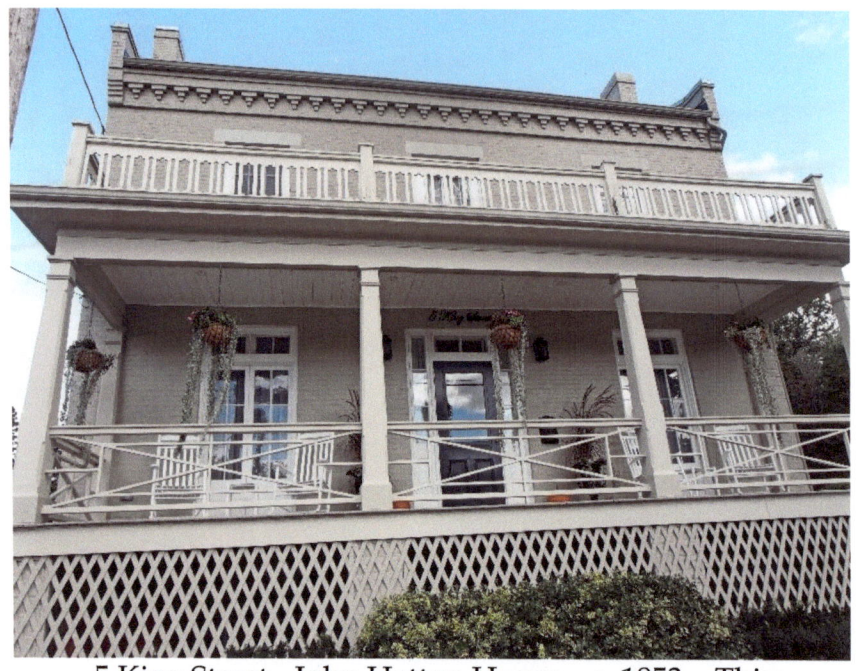

5 King Street - John Hatton House – c. 1853 – This house is a vernacular style with elements of Georgian and Regency. It has a centre hall plan, two full-length first and second storey verandahs on front, French doors in both living and dining rooms; formerly it had a belvedere on the roof.

John Hatton was a storekeeper on Walton Street in 1851, and by 1857, he had moved his store to Mill Street and was now a wholesale grocer. He appears in early assessments of Port Hope dating to 1822.

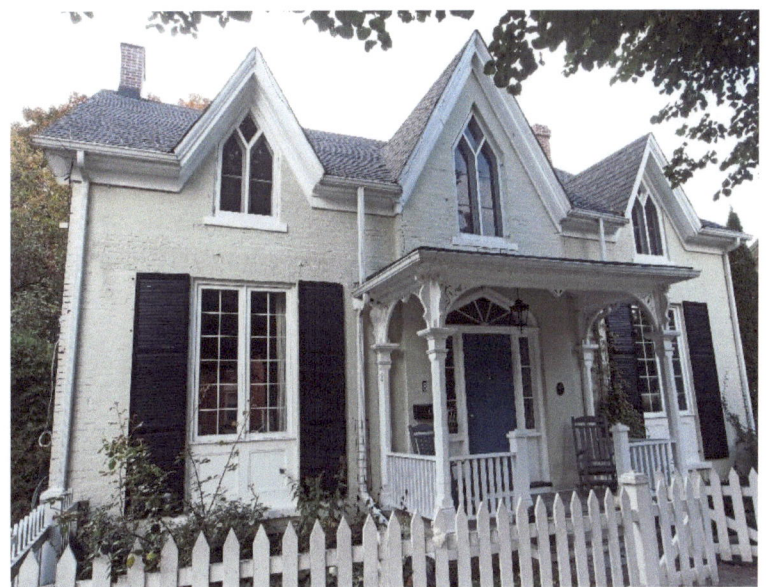

8 King Street - Robert Mitchell House – c. 1850 - This one and a half storey Gothic cottage has three bays to the ground floor, and is constructed of brick laid in Flemish bond with a coarse rubble foundation. The steep pitch of the gable roof, and the three steeply pointed gables containing pointed windows are distinguishing Gothic characteristics. The French doors on the ground floor and the front door with sidelights and ogre transom are typical of the Regency style. On the gable ends of the house are returned eaves. The porch in front of the main entrance, with its carved detail is a later addition.

Robert Mitchell (1799-1865) was a carpenter. Originally from Ireland, he arrived in Port Hope in the early 1830s. As an active member of the early Methodist congregation, he along with builder Phillip Fox constructed the first frame Methodist Church located on Brown Street in 1833 (on a lot across the street from the present church.)

His brother, William Mitchell (1799-1871), who was also a carpenter, resided in a dwelling a few doors to the south of Robert's house. Robert's children established businesses in Port Hope and were prominent merchants.

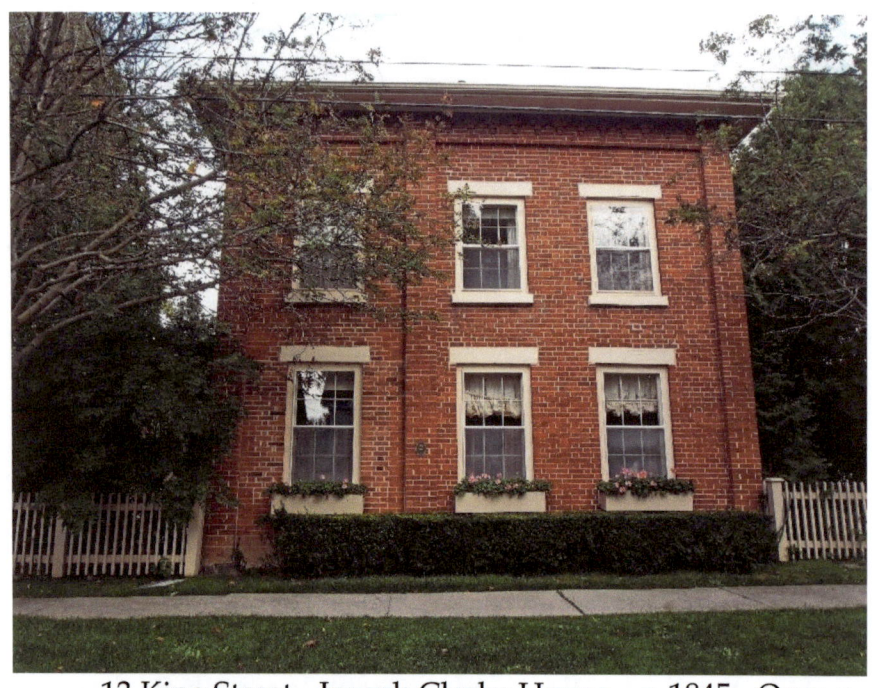

13 King Street - Joseph Clarke House – c. 1845 - Once a
flat-topped townhouse, this home has been capped by a
steeply pitched hipped roof. The eaves project and house a
plain-boxed cornice. All the structural openings in this
common-bond brick structure are set in recessed wall panels.
The panels are separated by pilasters, which run up through
the stepped decorative bricking found under the eaves. Most
of the windows are two panes over two set in flat openings
with wooden lugsills and heavy lintels.

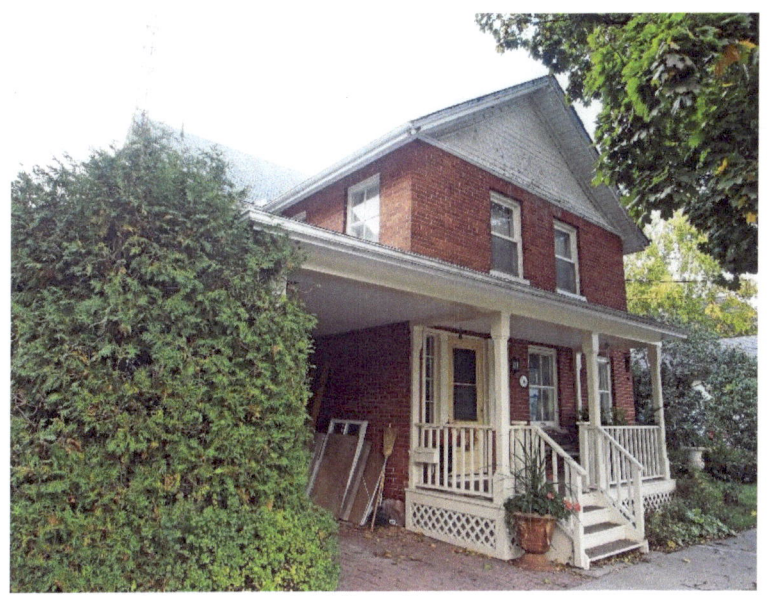

16 King Street

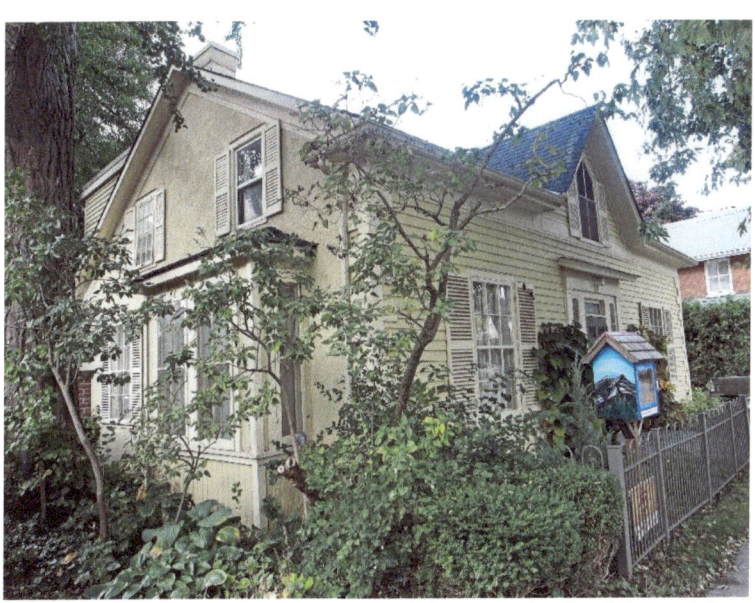

18 King Street – c. 1830s - saltbox with Gothic gable

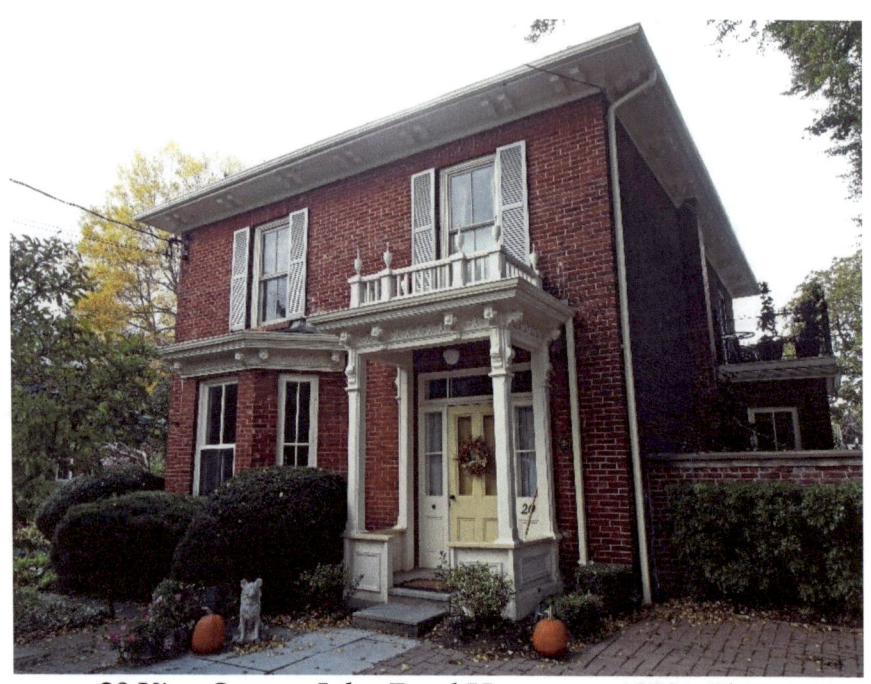

20 King Street - John Read House – c. 1870 - This two-storey house is clad in brick laid in an unusual pattern exhibiting paired headers between the normal stretcher pattern. This is similar to a type known as garden wall bond. The house has a low-pitched hipped roof with projecting eaves. Under the eaves lie pairs of tooled "S" brackets on a moulded frieze.

The window openings are flat and are headed by a brick radiating voussoir. The front facade top-storey windows have brick sills, which have replaced the wooden lugsills that sit below all of the home's other windows. The front facade has a one storey bay window with a hipped roof and eaves jutting out. A moulded corona decorates the plain cornice. Beneath this are medallioned block brackets set on a molded frieze panel which has been intricately decorated with carved swirling medallions.

The main entrance is framed by a flat-topped portico which is highly decorated in the same fashion as the bay and is supported further by carved brackets and bevelled posts. A molded panel encloses the bottom portion of the portico. The main entrance is a panelled door flanked by sidelights and headed by a flush, light transom panel.

A one-storey side addition has pilasters, which run to the eave line of the balcony above. A molded and panelled balustrade capped by round urns encloses the balcony. Underneath the eaves one can see decorative stepped brickwork.

John Read (1798-1886) was born in Dublin, Ireland and emigrated to Port Hope circa 1830. In 1853, he was a Town Inspector overseeing the By-Laws of the Municipal Council regarding liquor licensing.

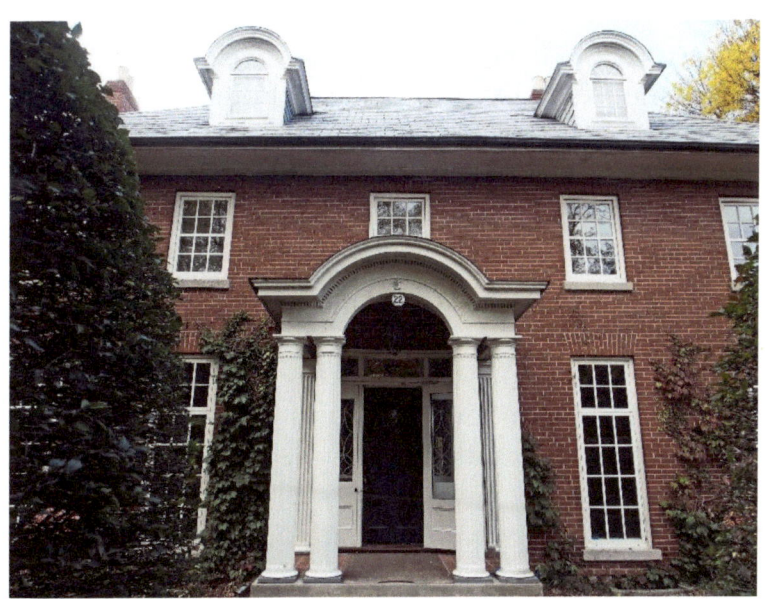

22 King Street – sidelights, transom, multipaned windows

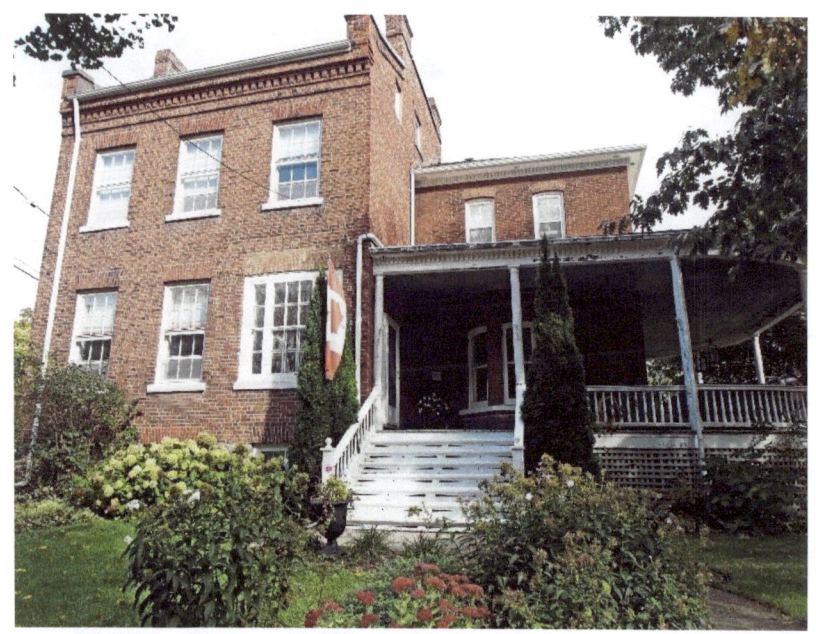

33 King Street - William M. Smith House – c. 1848 - This three bay, two storey brick house stands over a high basement, once the kitchen. Notable as an example of a Port Hope town house, its exterior detail includes a finely executed ornamental frieze in brick, parapet walls, with twin chimneys, and panelled piers forming the lower ends. Raking sections of parapets have projecting string and cap courses. South chimneys still have original corbelled caps. The windows have original sash of six panes over six of twelve by eighteen-inch glass.

The house is now a composite with a turn of the century addition to the south end, also two stories, and built of brick. This has a verandah across the west front and down the south side, its plan with curved corners and its denticulated frieze typical of the period. This addition has a front bay window lighting the new drawing room. The change represented by this addition also altered the original front entrance to the side opening off the veranda.

In 1848, Dr. William Miller Smith, the fifth son of John David Smith, builder of the Bluestone (21 Dorset Street East) built the left or townhouse portion of this house.

Dr. William Miller Smith (1815-1854) married Charlotte Ward (1824-1852), the youngest daughter of Judge Thomas Ward in 1841. William was the only son of John David Smith who pursued a career in medicine. In 1852, he was a Board Member of the Harbour Commissioners along with his brothers, John Shuter Smith and E.P. Smith who was Chairman.

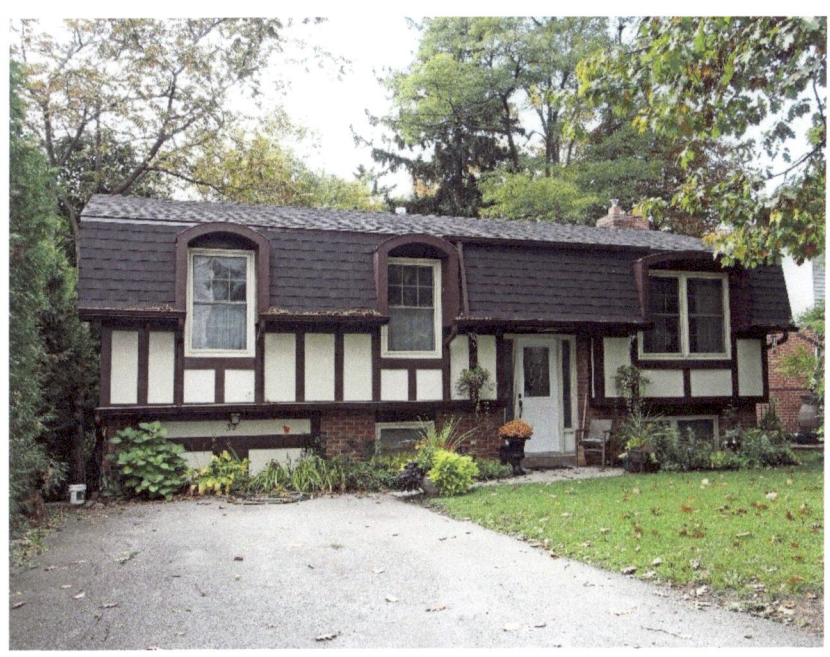

King Street

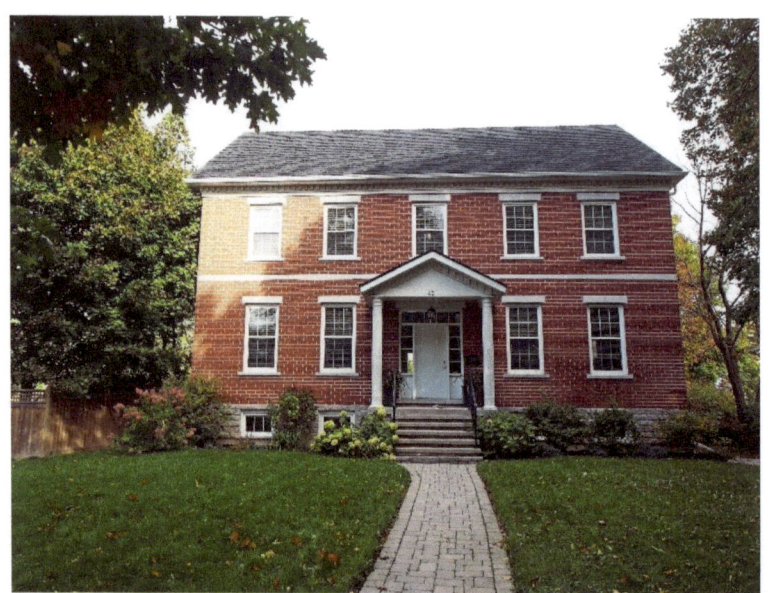

43 King Street – Georgian – multipaned windows, sidelights, transom, pediment

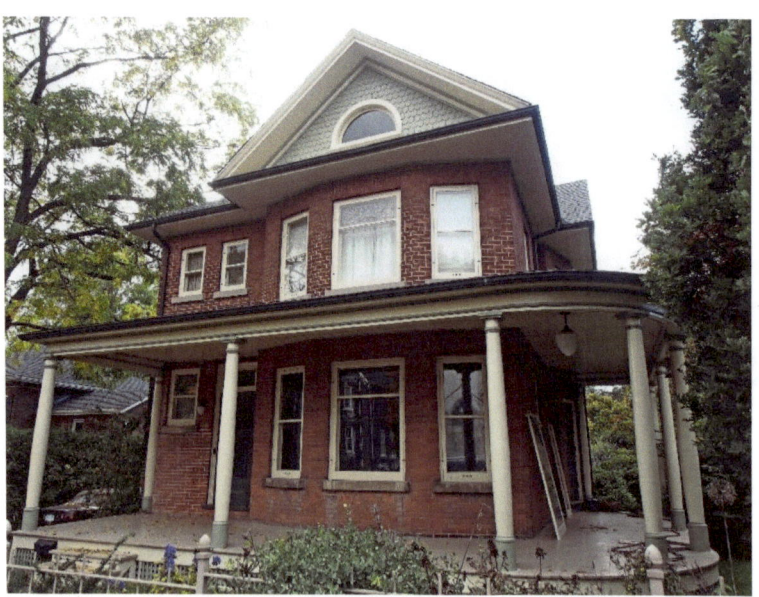

King Street – wraparound veranda

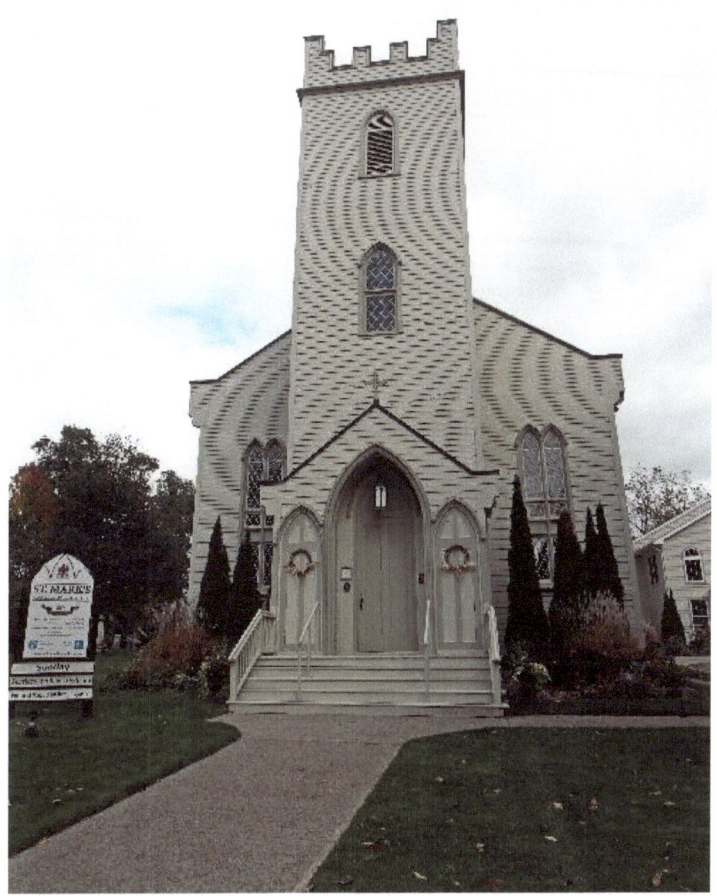

51 King Street – St. Mark's Anglican Church – built in 1822 – With an enlargement in 1842 and alteration to windows and tower in 1851, the church approached its present size, form and Gothic appearance. On July 25, 1959, Her Majesty, Queen Elizabeth II, and His Royal Highness Prince Philip accompanied their host the Right Honourable Vincent Massey, Governor General of Canada and a parishioner of St. Mark's to morning worship here.

It has Gothic windows and door arches and a battlemented tower.

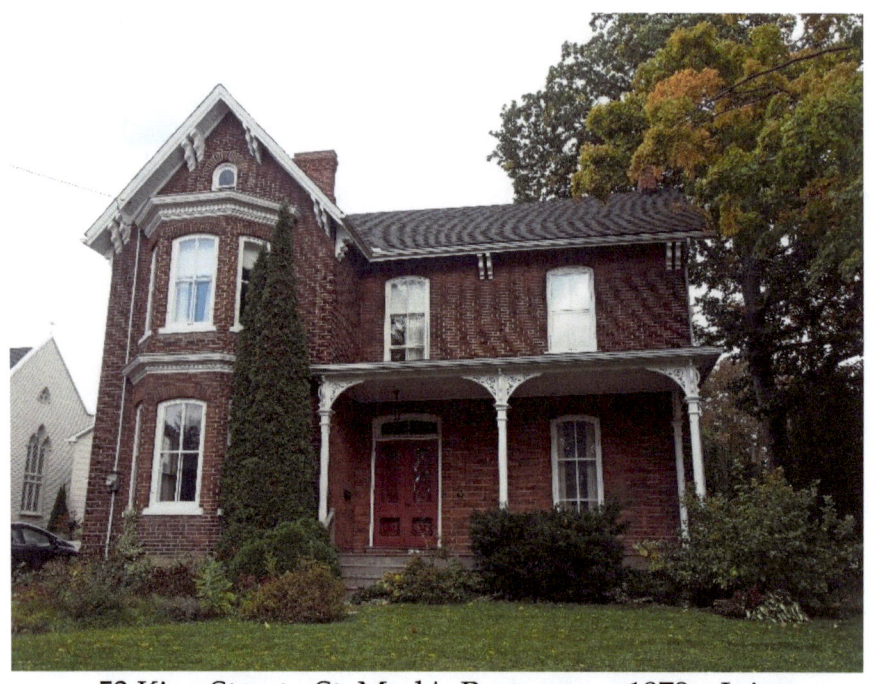

53 King Street - St. Mark's Rectory – c. 1878 – It is a good example of the late Victorian villa with Italianate details in red brick complete with its essential exterior details of two storey bay window, paired brackets to eaves, and gables, elaborate front verandah, Victorian sashing and entrance door case.

In 1956, St. Mark's Church sold the Ambrose House (50 King Street) in order to purchase this house located directly beside the Church for use as a rectory.

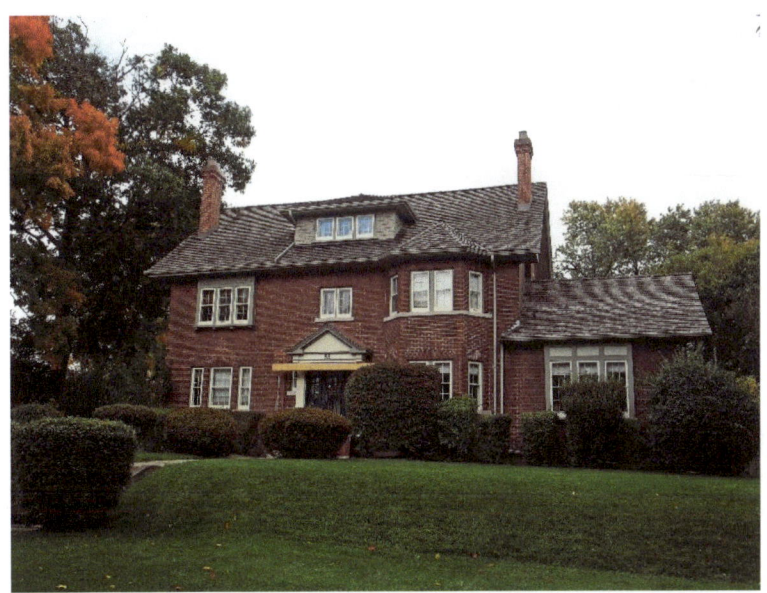

55 King Street - Charles Wickett House – c. 1909 - This house was built for Charles Hearn Wickett, a prominent dry goods merchant. About1920 the first floor was extended to the south and the back verandah added. It is side gabled, three storeys, triple brick, stretcher bond on a cement foundation. It has an irregular cedar shake roof, gables half timbered on stucco, hooded windows and dormers. The fenestration is the most impressive feature with a total of 47 multi-faceted windows in a variety of groupings.

Except for the neoclassical front entrance and back verandah this house is an interesting Canadian vernacular version of the Arts and Crafts style of architecture.

The house has a symmetrical plan with a large hall, three reception rooms, a large kitchen and butler's pantry on the main floor, four bedrooms plus a sewing room and bathroom on the second, and another three bedrooms and bathroom on the third. In 1912, the living room was enlarged by extending the main floor at the front to the south. In the space created behind the extension a two-sided verandah was added.

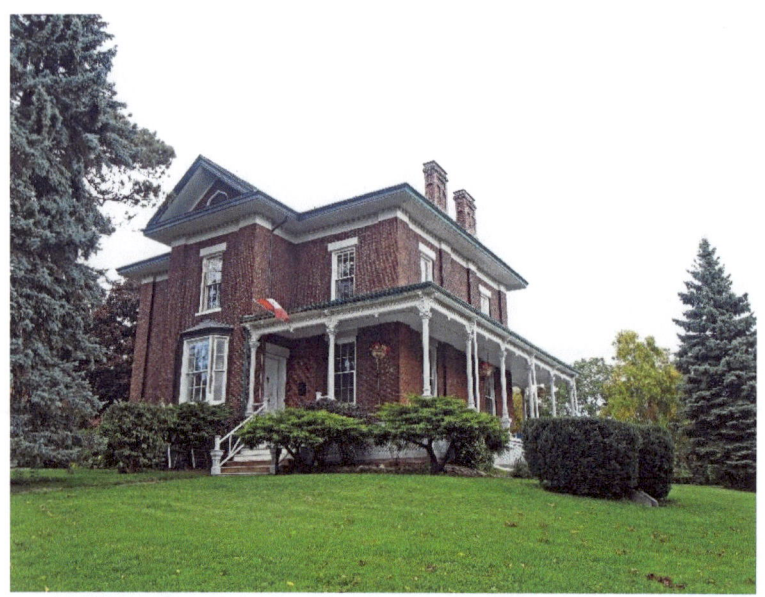

61 King Street - R. Charles Smith House – c. 1858 - The house is basically a hip roof Regency Villa with a central hall plan. The main west facade is relieved by a central projection with a pedimental gable, and pilasters, articulating the south wall and each corner, enhance the mass and solidity of the structure. Decorative projecting header bricks under the wide eaves resemble dentils. The two tall brick chimneys on each side of the house are ornamented with brick dentils and with recessed panels. A verandah spans the south side of the house and has eight-sided posts resting on panelled square bases, and carved details below the roof line. There is a bay window in the frontispiece consisting of one six over six, and two two-over-two double hung sash.

Robert Charles Smith (1817-1886) built this impressive brick house for himself and his wife Sara. The house is across the street from his father's house (John David Smith), the Bluestone (21 Dorset Street East). In 1851, R. Charles Smith contributed to the building boom that occurred during the early 1850s by building a commercial block at 48-60 Walton Street. He established himself as a lumber dealer.

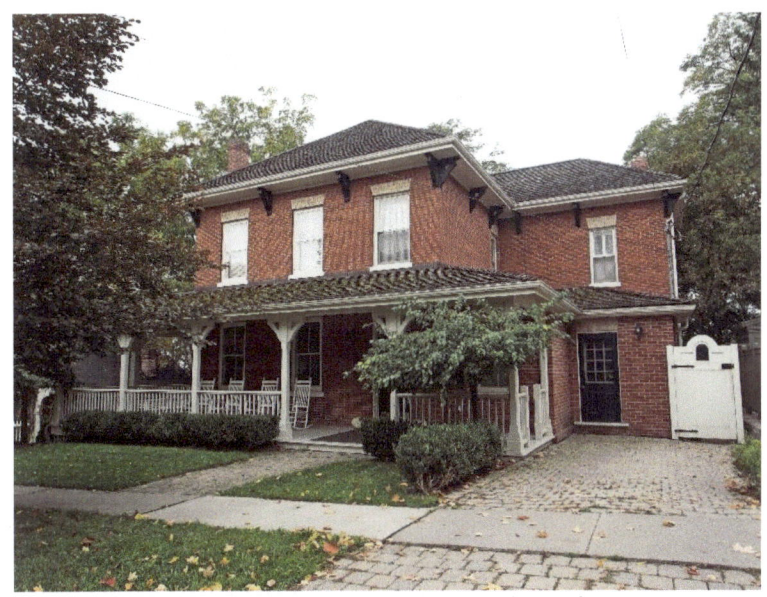

56 King Street – hipped roof

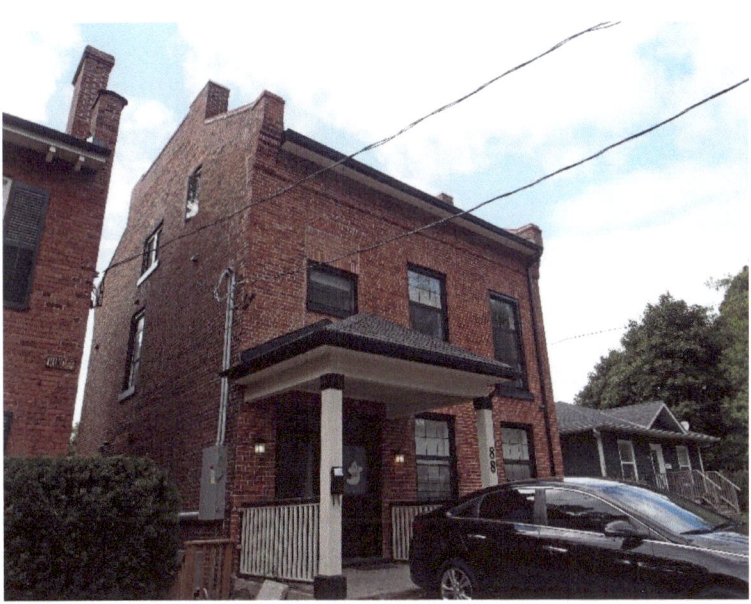

88 King Street

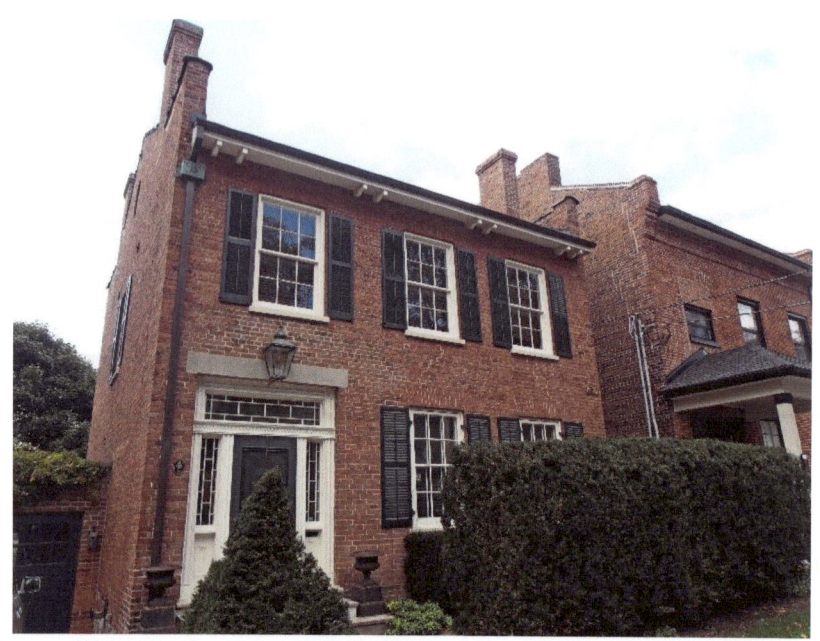

92 King Street - Smith House – c. 1845 - The exterior is a two-storey brick front (three storey back split) of a town-house style with a low pitch gabled roof parallel to King Street. The building has parapet walls at the north and south ends with four prominent chimneys extending from the parapet walls. Three of the chimneys were originally working, the fourth is strictly decorative.

The five-bay front has three windows above and two below with the third opening at the extreme left being the doorway. Windows on street level have either stone or concrete sills with brick lintels. The doorway is elaborate with blocked corners and a lintel decoration on the outside below the transom. The transom and sidelights consist of a large brick of glass surrounded entirely by small bricks of glass. The mouldings consist of a wide oval and two side mouldings each side of this. Together these form a column which is terminated by corner blocks which separate transom, door and sidelights. Below the sidelights is a heavy panel matching that of the door and trim.

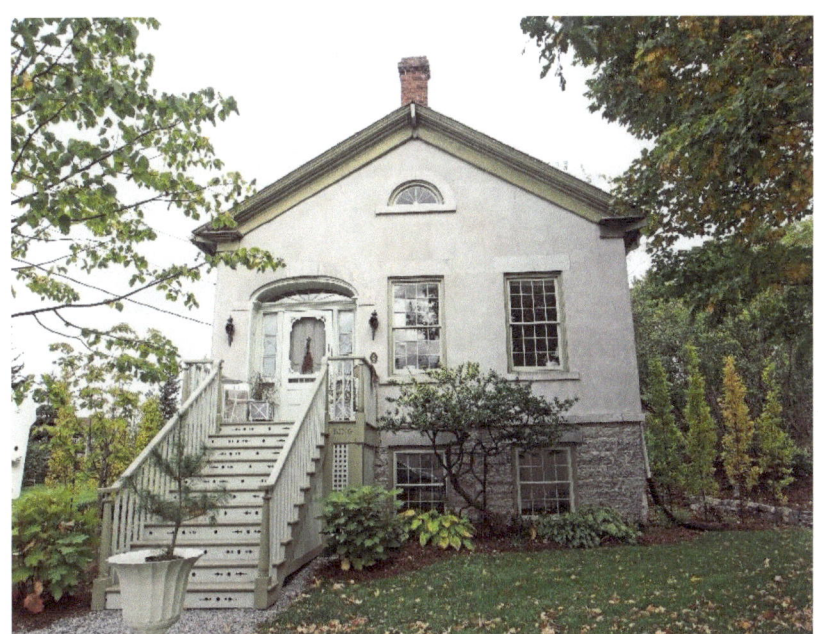

117 King Street - Elias Peter Smith House (The Little Bluestone) – c. 1834 - The little Bluestone is a small Upper Canadian house, little more than a cottage. Certain elements are related to the Bluestone, but here the local stone also stuccoed is supplemented by limestone of better quality for sills, lintels and string course instead of the red sandstone used in the larger house. The principal external feature which gives such distinction to the facade is the door case, but its dominance over the adjoining windows is relieved by the judiciously placed semi-circular attic light in the gable.

In 1834, John David Smith married his second wife Augusta and built the Bluestone (21 Dorset Street East). In that same year, J.D. Smith's eldest son, Elias Peter Smith (1807-1860) married Sophia Soper (1803-1885) and the Little Bluestone was built on the same estate.

Elias Peter Smith was named after his grandfather, Elias Smith, one of the founding fathers of Port Hope. He was the Manager of the local branch of the Bank of Upper Canada located in the 1840's on Walton Street (118-120 Walton Street).

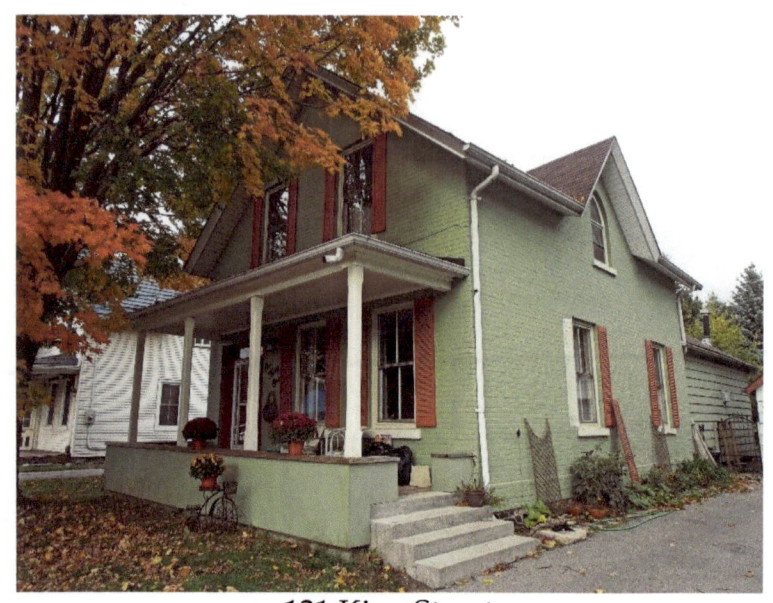

121 King Street

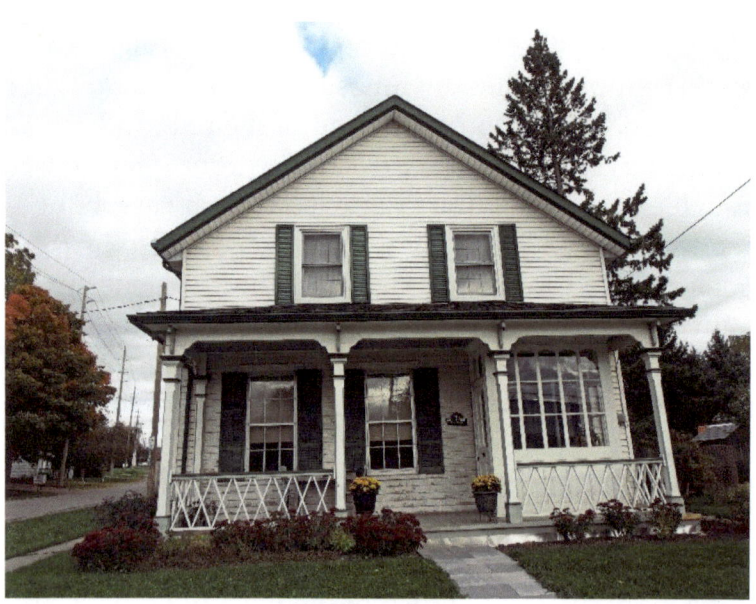

123 King Street

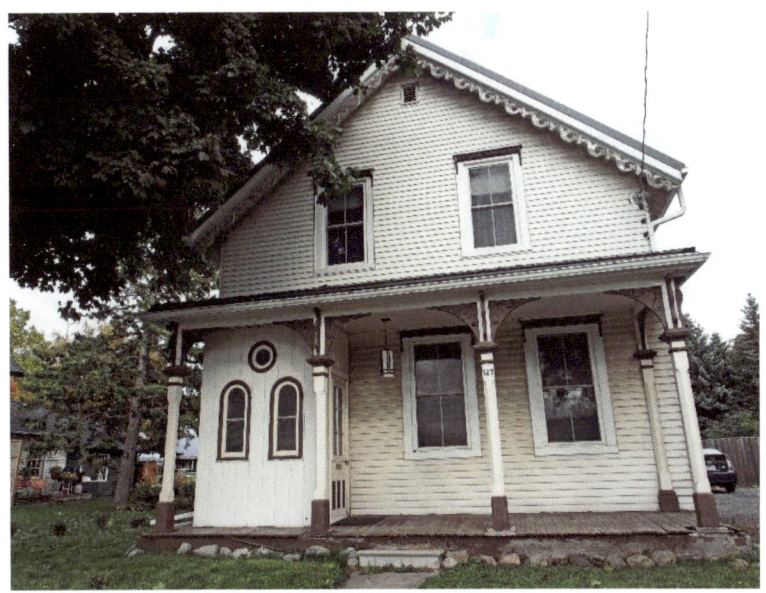

127 King Street

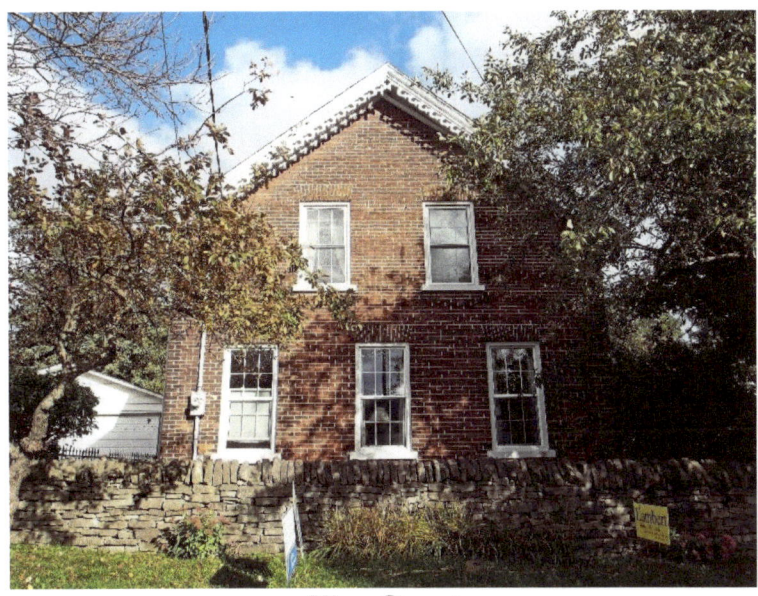

King Street

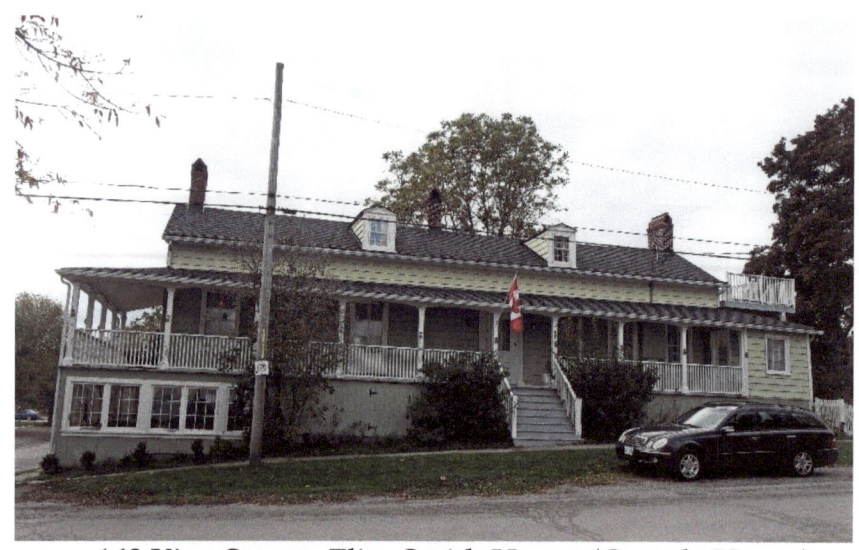

168 King Street - Elias Smith House (Canada House) – c. 1800 - It is Port Hope's oldest building. Built by founder Elias Smith this house also served as a school and post office during construction. Eventually it became a seaman's inn.

This original inn is typical of early Upper Canada architecture. It is a frame story and a half house, post and beam construction with symmetrically placed six over six and twelve over twelve windows. There are seven dormers with moderate details and hand-hewn eaves troughs. The large chimney gives hints of the importance of the hearth and cooking device so central to early Upper Canada life. The strong foundation is built of two feet thick beach stones.

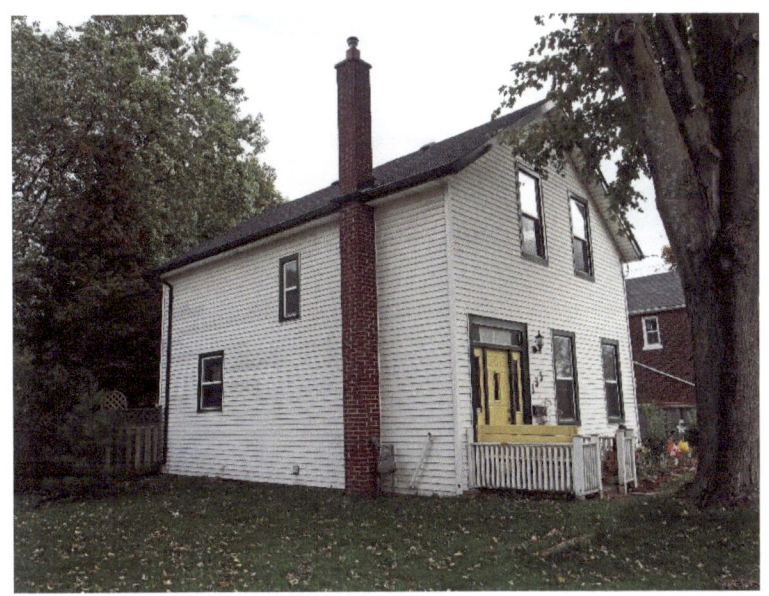

135 King Street

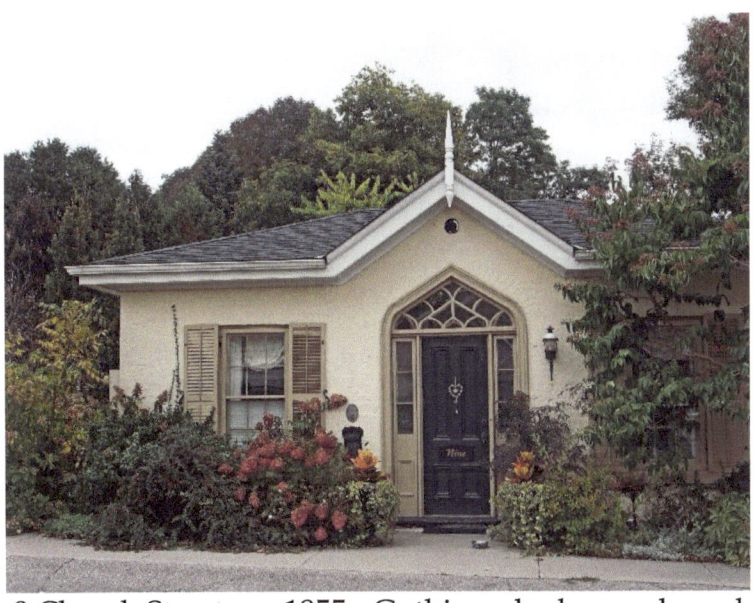

9 Church Street – c. 1855 - Gothic arched ogee shaped
transom, sidelights, finial on gable

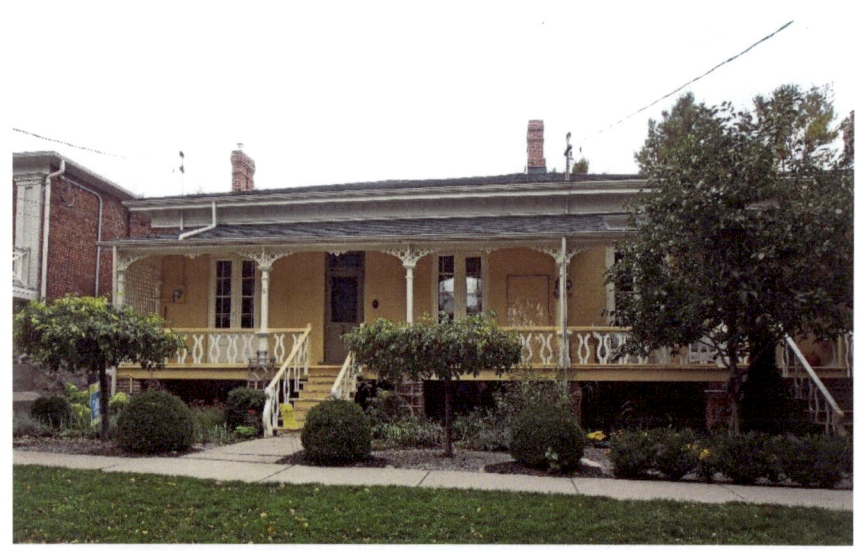

4-6 Baldwin Street - Robert Youdan Terrace – c. 1853

4 Baldwin Street may be described as a semidetached, two storey (second storey at ground level), three bay house built in the Regency Cottage style. It has a low-hipped roof and a boxed cornice with frieze and brackets. The three-panel front door with simple sash, unglazed transom and panelled embrasure is flanked by pairs of French windows. A fine gallery runs along the front of both this house and its almost identical semi-detached neighbour, 6 Baldwin Street, with lyre-shaped supports on the railing very similar to those at Barrett's Terrace. The present two sections of the semi-detached structure were built a few years apart as indicated by the brickwork and structural details. The unit on the east side (#4) was built first.

Robert Youdan was born in England in 1812 and later became a resident of Port Hope. His skills as a mason and builder were much required during Port Hope's building boom of the 1850s.

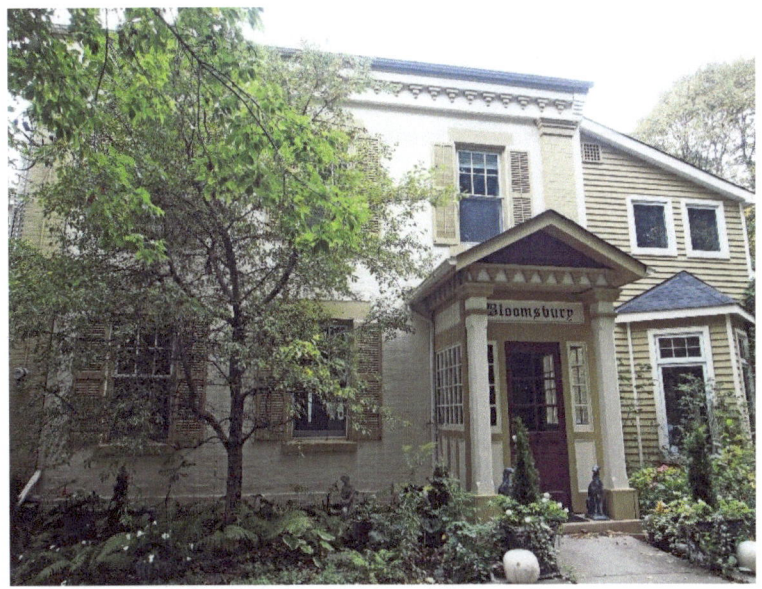

2 Baldwin Street – Bloomsbury

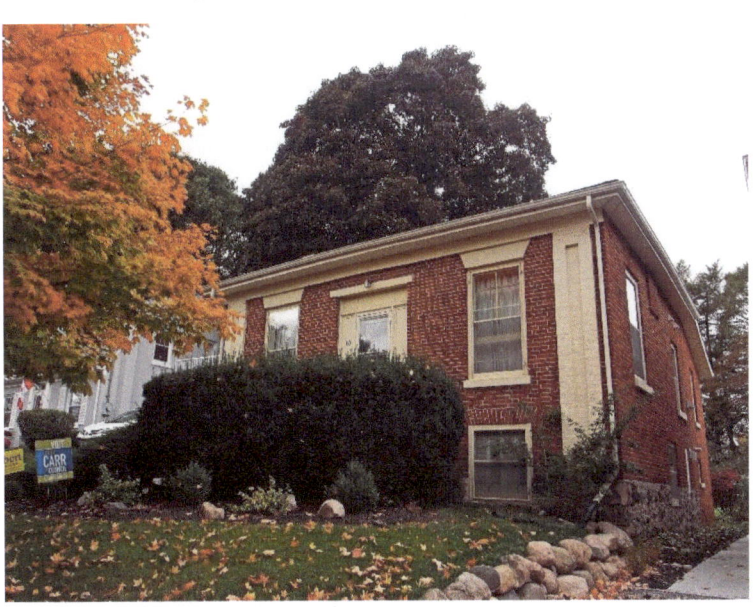

10 Baldwin Street

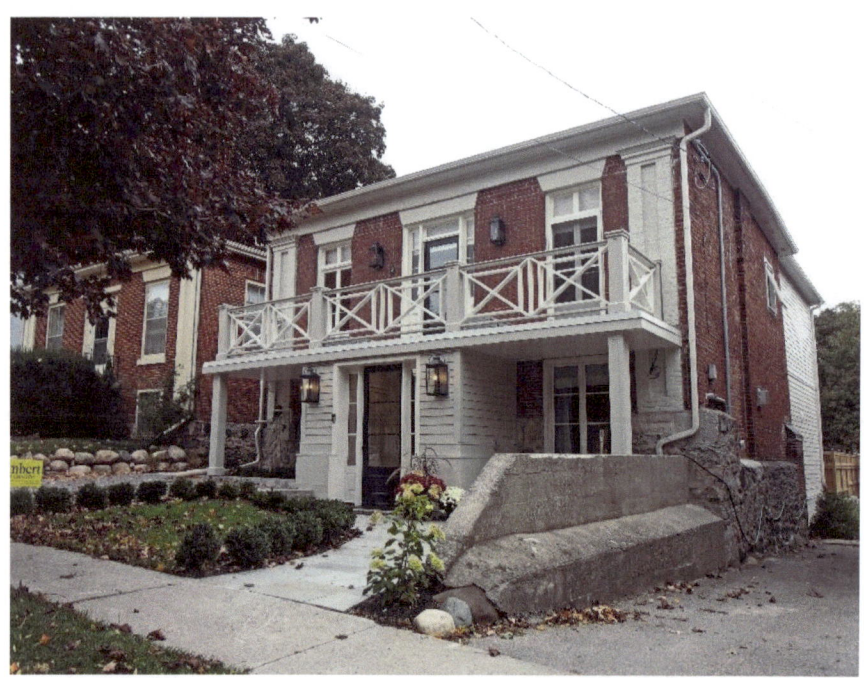

8 Baldwin Street – Ontario Regency Cottage – c. 1860 - Its hipped roof and main storey set on a high basement offer the amenity of a full two-storey house somewhat more capacious than the alternative storey and a half arrangement. The design is a three-bay front in red brick notable for its twin pilaster corner treatment, French windows, and centre door case with full height sidelights and transom above the door. The brickwork starts at the sill level of the lower storey windows and the pilasters are terminated by a projecting brick frieze across the front of the building below the soffit of the eaves. Lower windows are casements in pairs to main room with timber lintels of flat arch outline.

The two-level verandah is a twentieth century rebuilding of an earlier arrangement of similar form. Front walls enclosing the lower storey are also more recent work. Pilasters are painted a contrasting buff colour.

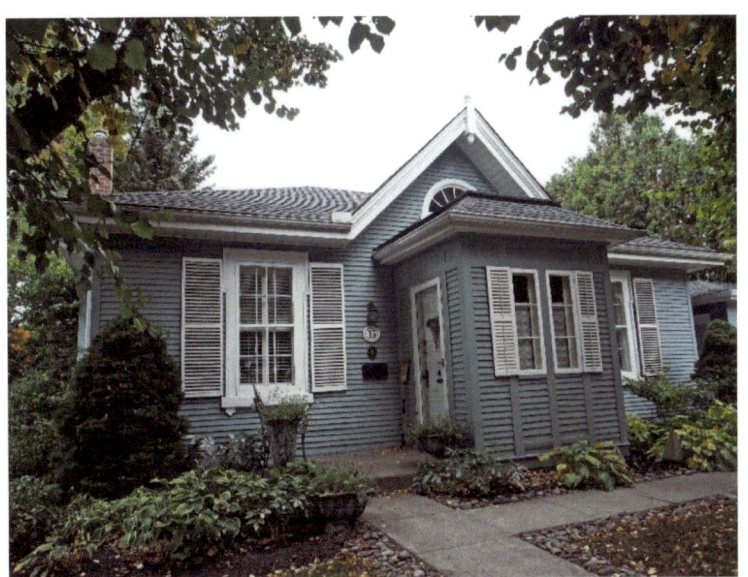

15 Baldwin Street - William Hewson House – c. 1850 -
This is a one-storey cottage from the north facade, while a
view of the south facade shows two storeys. It is a classic
example of the Ontario Cottage with three bays and a centre
gable in its hipped roof. The house is done in narrow
clapboard. The building has well-proportioned exterior
features and a centre-hall plan. At the gable peak in the centre
of the main facade sits a finial; directly below this, tucked into
the gable, is a semi-circular fanlight divided into five parts by
narrow radiating muntins.

Between the main facade's windows and directly below
the fanlight is a small, enclosed porch. Small double windows
of three panes each are located on the front face of the porch
which has a truncated hipped roof. The sashed windows are
six-over-six and have slightly protruding lugsills that are
decorated with end drops resembling acorns. The windows
are treated with eared label surrounds. The horizontally
louvred shutters on the main facade are for decoration.

15 and 11 Baldwin Street were built by William and
Henry Hewson. The Hewson brothers were born in England
and arrived in Port Hope in the early 1840s.

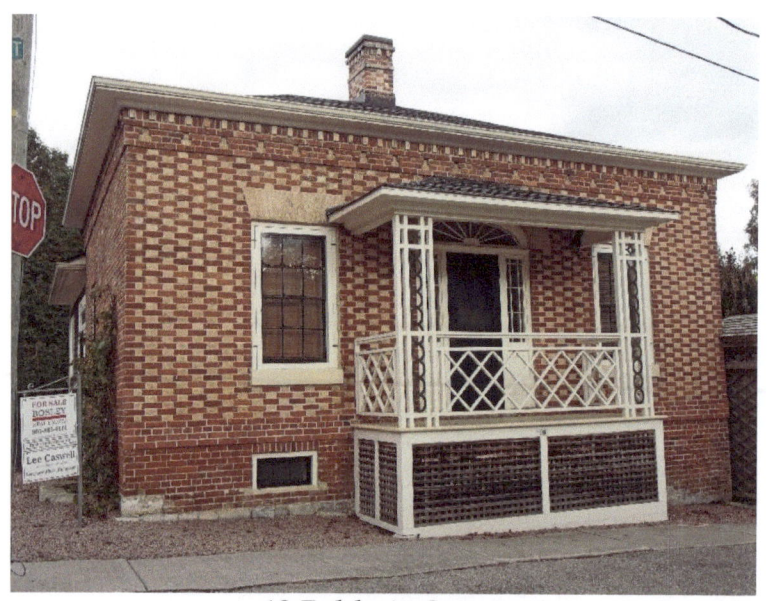

13 Baldwin Street

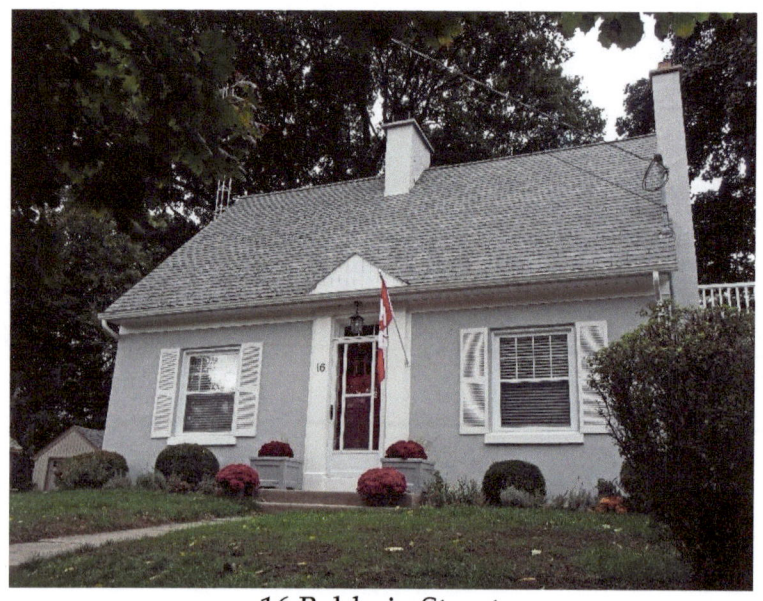

16 Baldwin Street

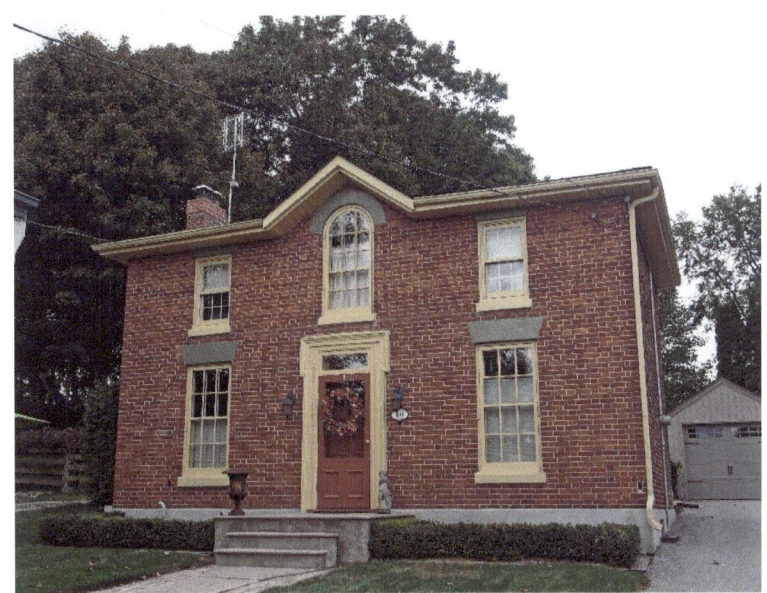

20 Baldwin Street

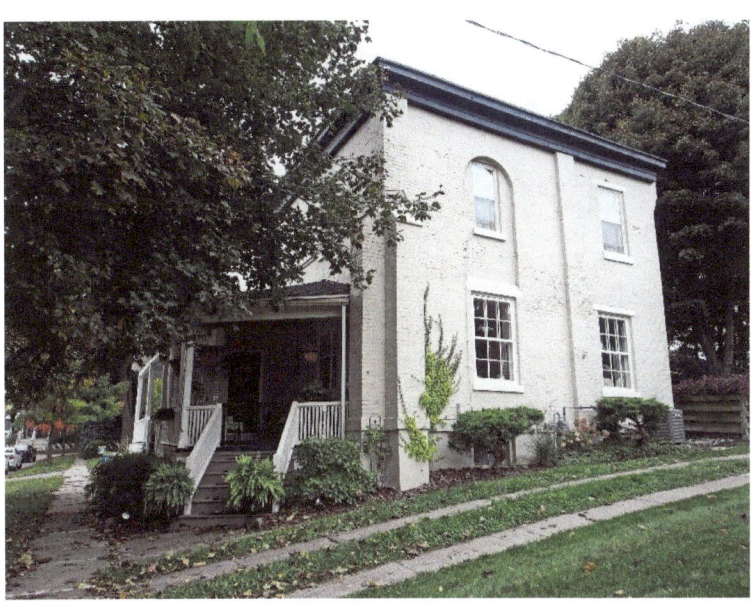

22 Baldwin Street

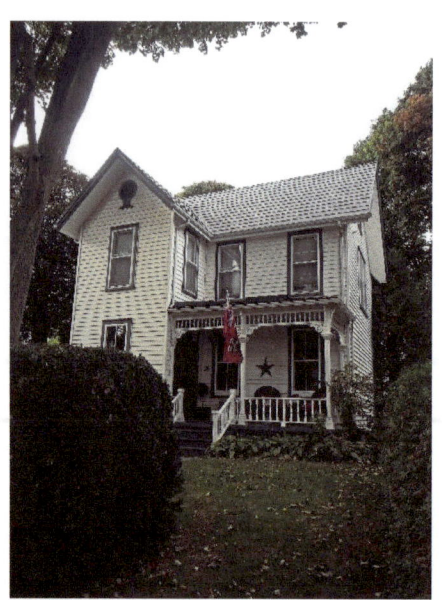

28 Baldwin Street

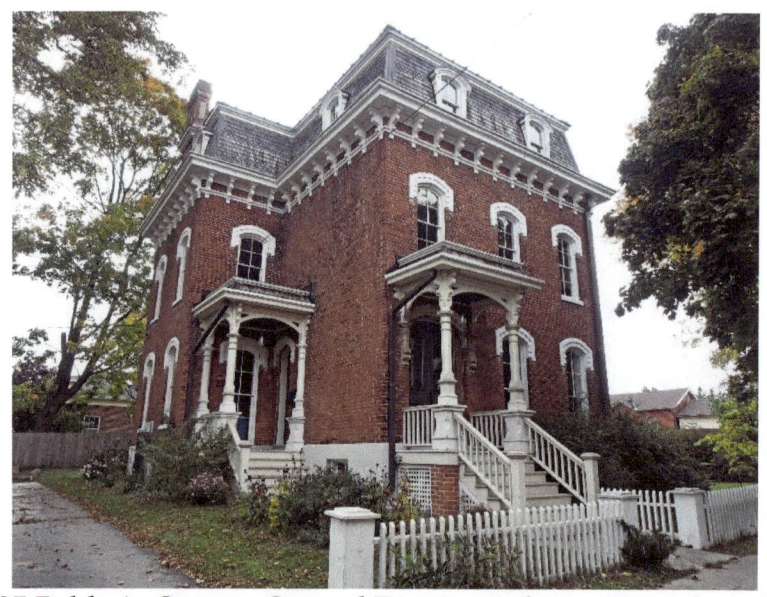

35 Baldwin Street – Second Empire style – mansard roof, cornice brackets, attractive porches, arched voussoirs

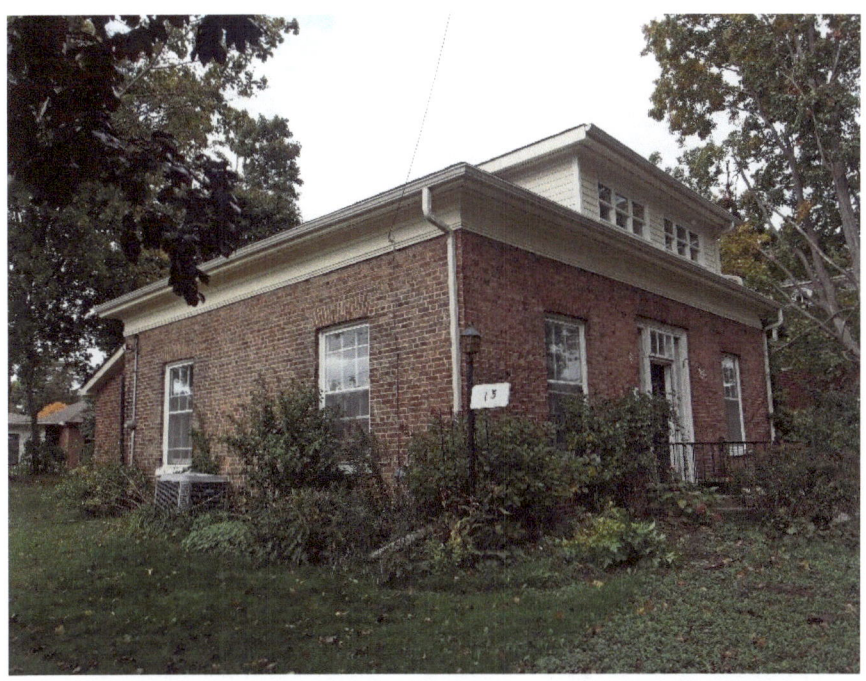

15 Julia Street - Cassie Cottage – c. 1852 – The Regency brick Cottage has one- and-one-half storeys, a centre door, and two large first floor windows on either side of the front door, and a low hip roof with two front dormers. It was built by Reverend John Cassie (1819-1861) who was the Minister of the First Presbyterian Church from 1835 until his death in 1861. He was a native of Aberdeenshire, Scotland.

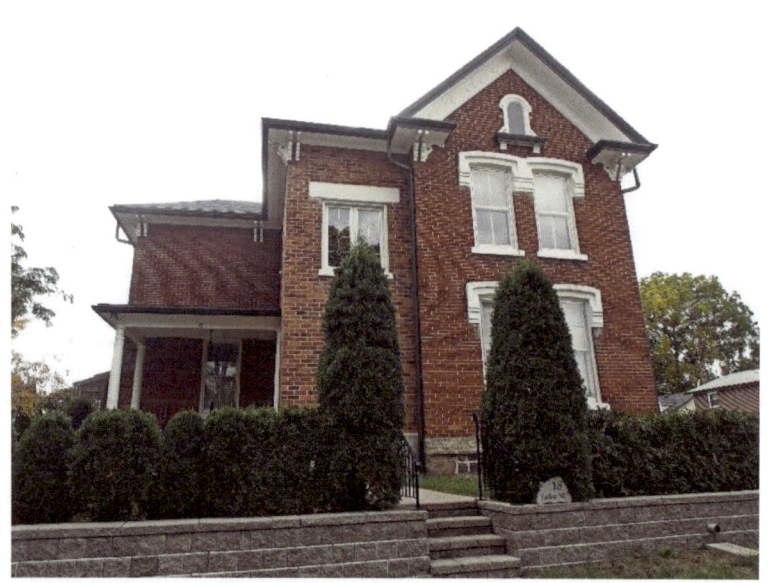

18 Julia Street – 2½-storey frontispiece, cornice brackets

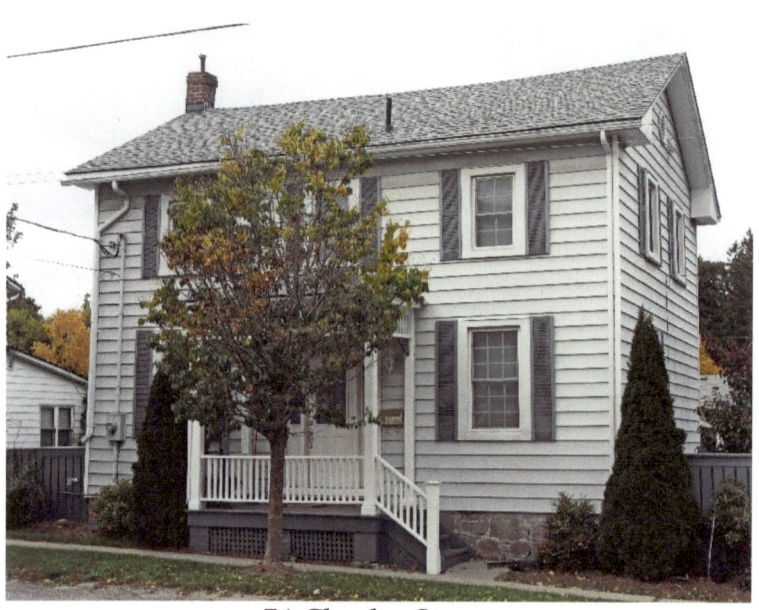

54 Charles Street

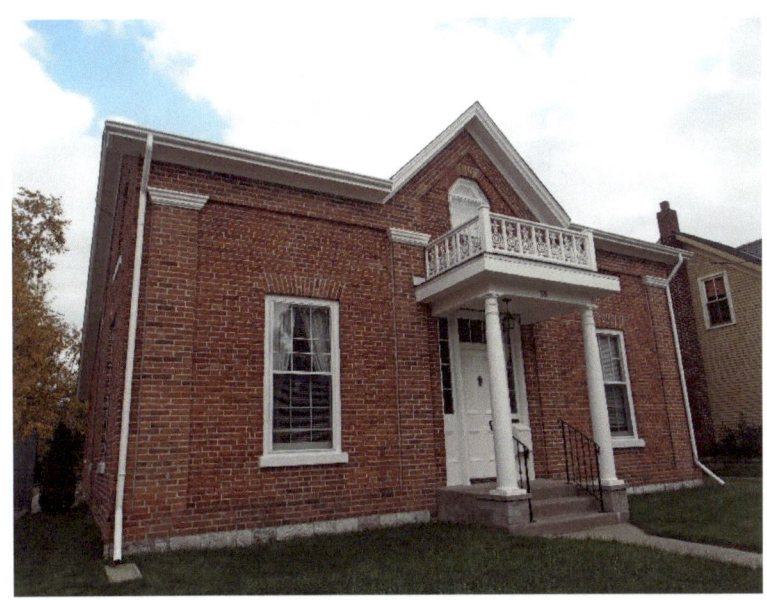

59 Charles Street – second floor balcony above entrance with sidelights and transom

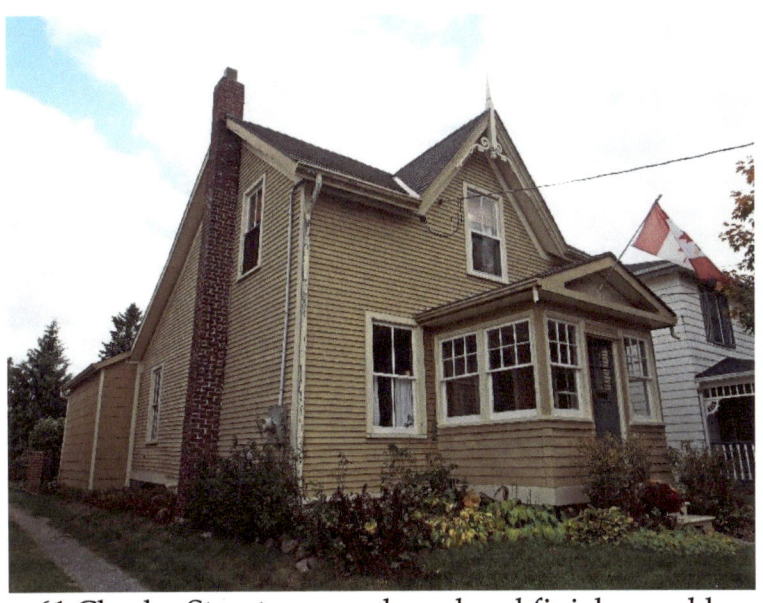

61 Charles Street – verge board and finial on gable

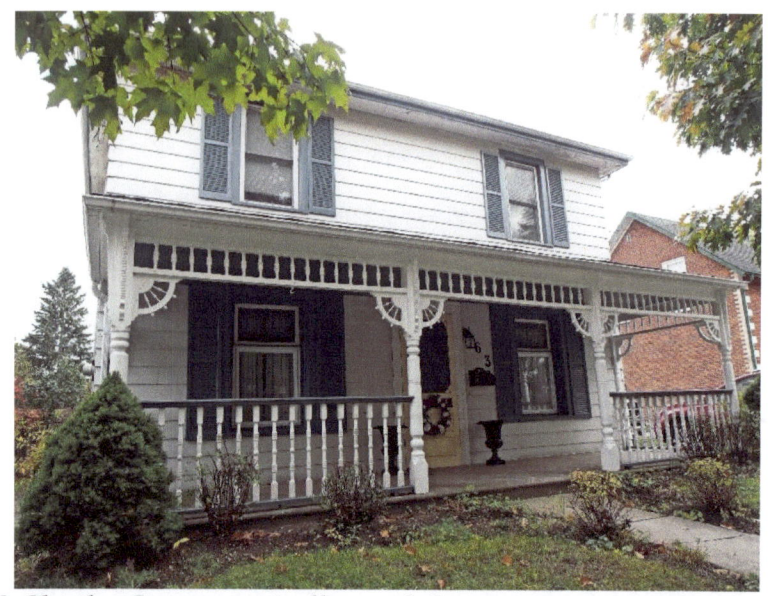

63 Charles Street – spindles and decorative work on turned porch supports

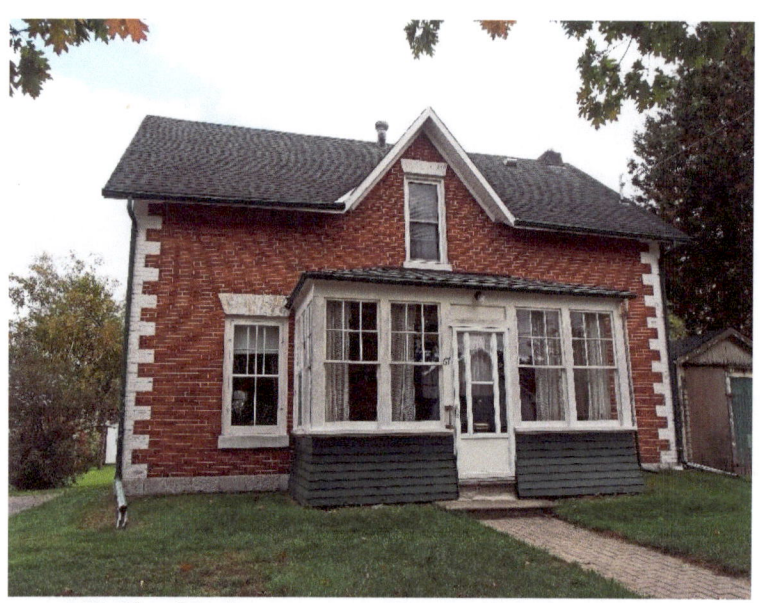

67 Charles Street – contrasting corner quoins

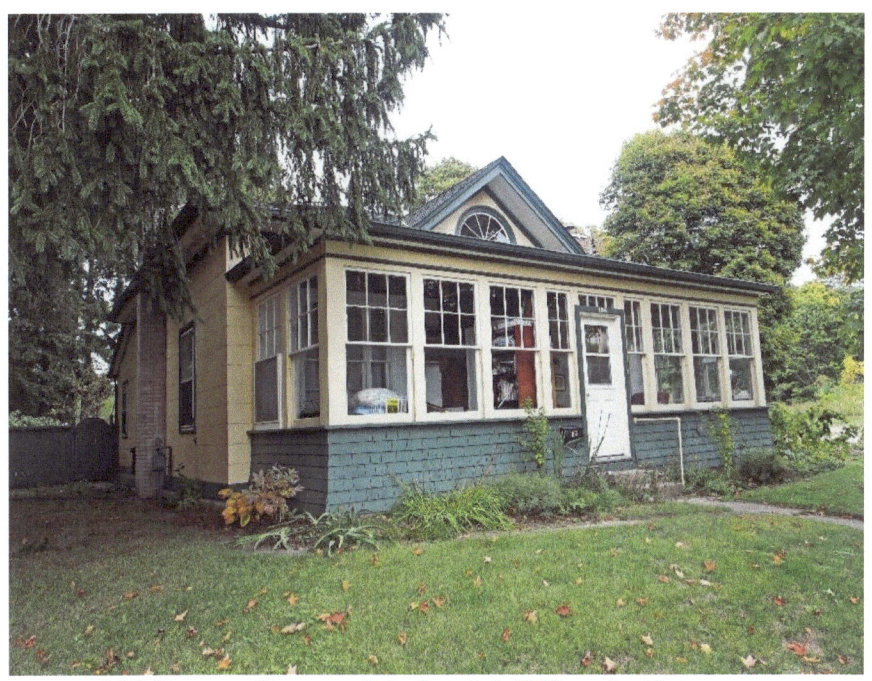

108 Bruton Street – Nathaniel Gillespie Cottage – c. 1854 – This is an Ontario Cottage, single storey frame house with a hipped roof and a semi-circular window in the central gable. the sun porch now masking the front is a more recent addition and may replace an earlier verandah, a feature to be expected on the south face.

Nathaniel Gillespie (1821-1899) was originally from County Armagh Ireland. He and his wife Cecelia emigrated to Canada in 1847. He established himself as a painter, during the building boom of the 1850s and it is an occupation he would have his entire life. The house remained in the Gillespie family, transferring to son Robert Tobias in 1899 after the death of both Nathaniel and Cecelia, which occurred within two days of each other.

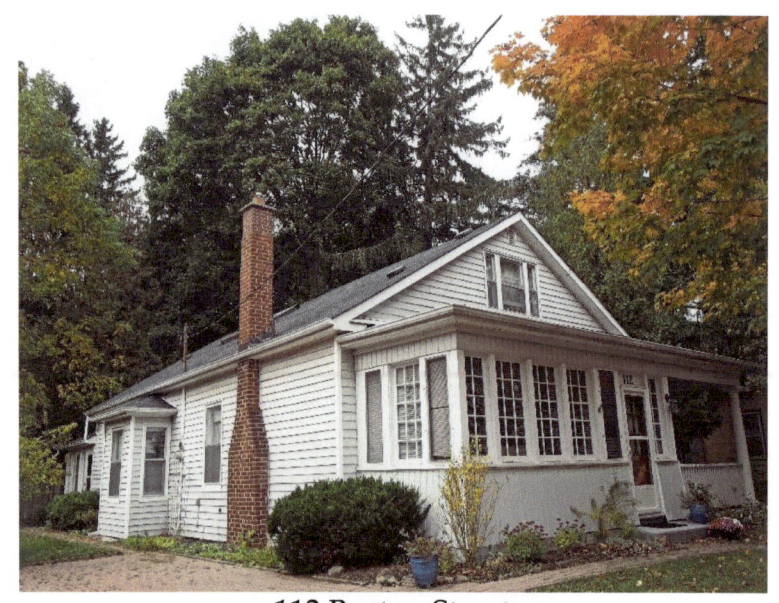

112 Bruton Street

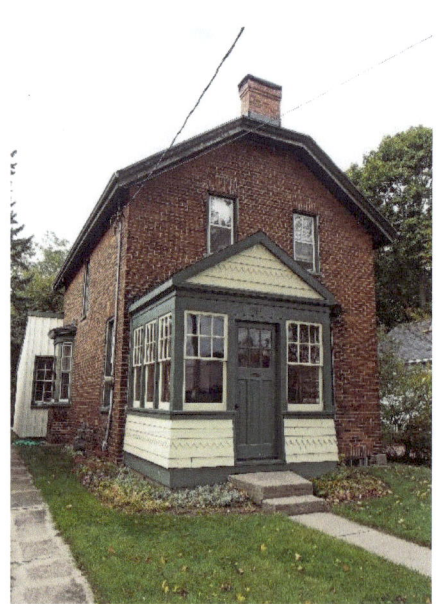

116 Bruton Street

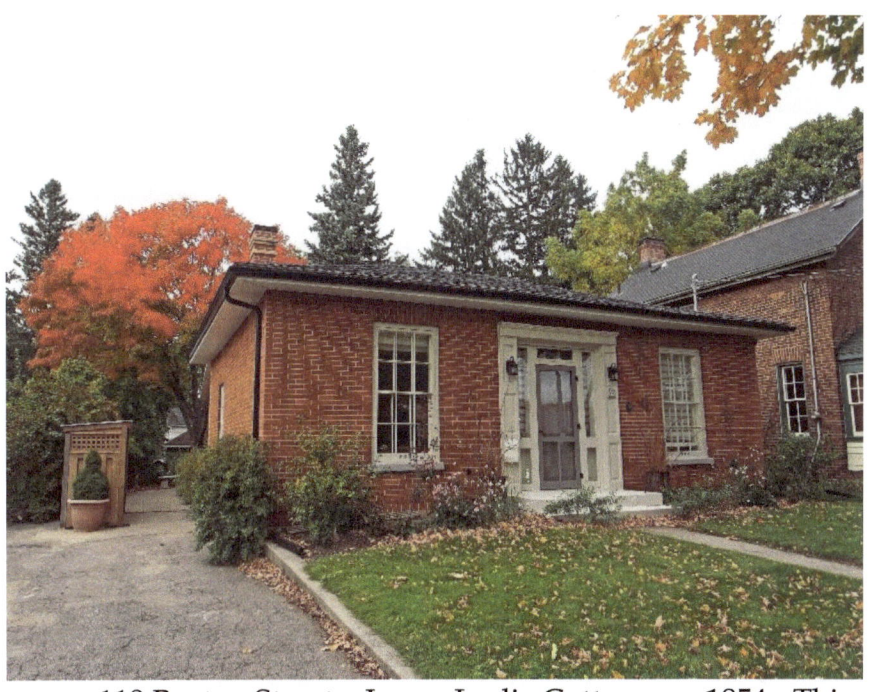

118 Bruton Street – James Leslie Cottage - c. 1854 - This is a simple one storey Ontario Cottage. The symmetrical front facade has two large six over six windows and a central door with sidelights.

James Leslie (1829-1904) was born in Ireland later emigrating to Canada. By 1851, he is listed as a plasterer residing on Bruton Street. In 1857, after the sale of the above property, he is listed as a plasterer residing on Sullivan Street.

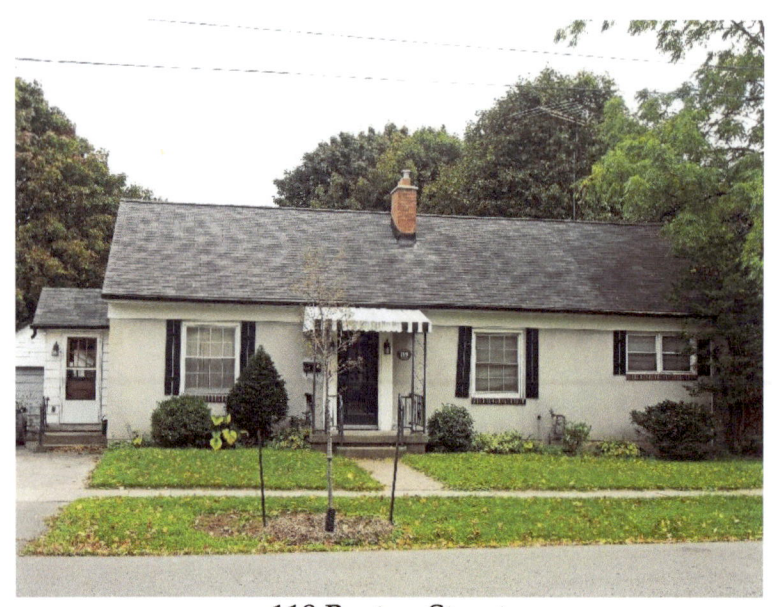

119 Bruton Street

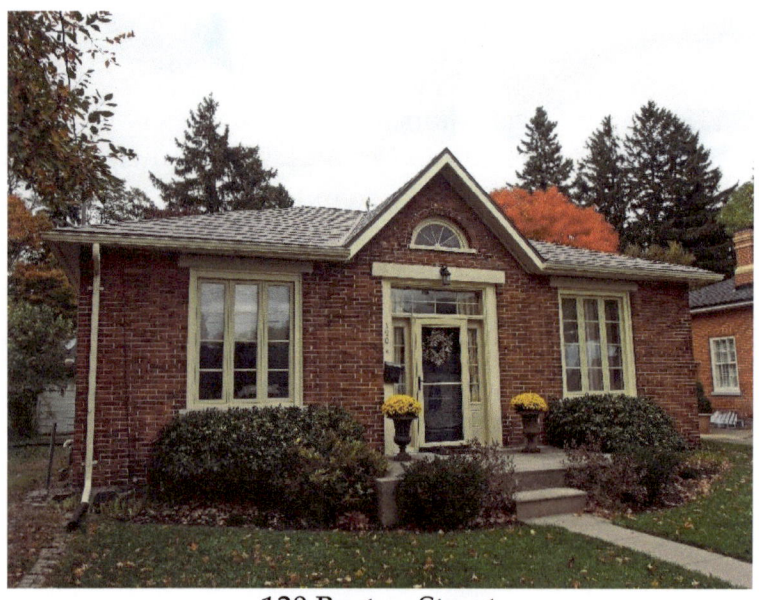

120 Bruton Street

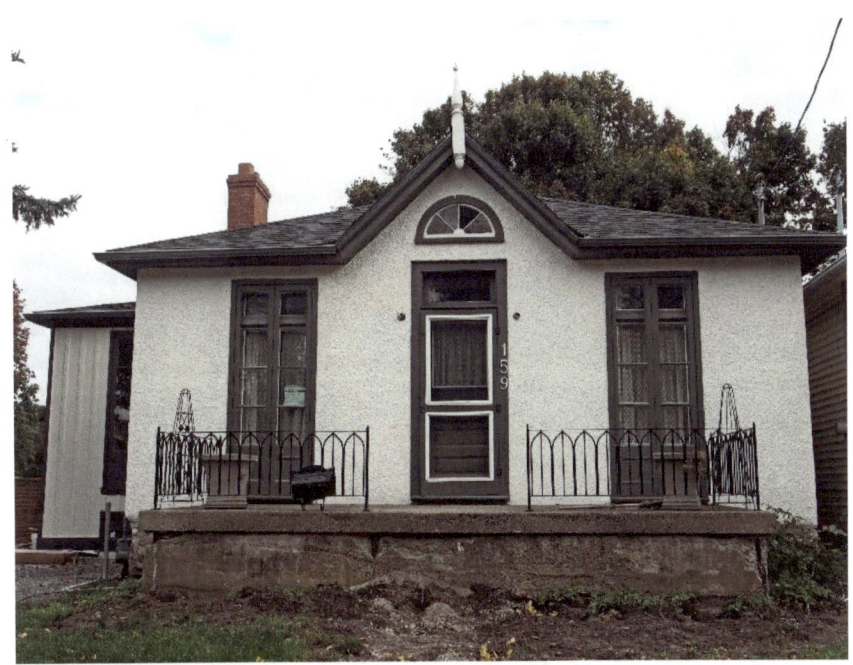

159 Bruton Street - William Skitch Cottage – c. 1861 - This is a diminutive example of the Ontario cottage with a hip roof, front gable with fanlight and end chimneys; the house is set over a high basement so that the rear allows more light to the cellar. The facade has a centre door with transom above flanked by French windows. The building has a rear wing. The exterior is rendered in roughcast, but there is evidence of the original stucco finish scored to look like ashlar.

William Skitch (1823-1894) was born in Stratton, Cornwall, England in 1823, emigrating to Canada in 1850. His wife, Anne Burney and five children arrived later that year. William established a tailoring business. Unfortunately, his shop was located in the Quinlan Block (78-92 Walton Street), which was destroyed by a fire in 1866. He was left with only his tailor irons as a result of not having any insurance. He was able to re-establish his business and by 1871, son Henry (1849-1924) was also a tailor. He took over the family business when William died in 1894.

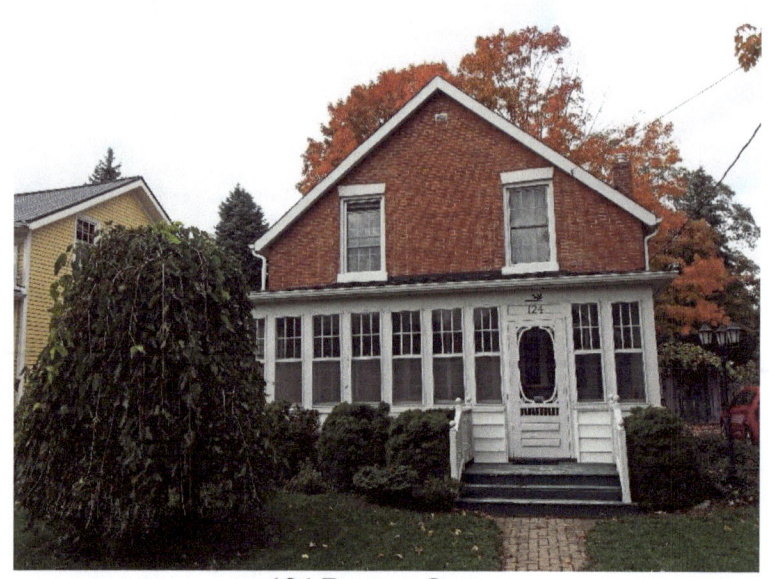

124 Bruton Street

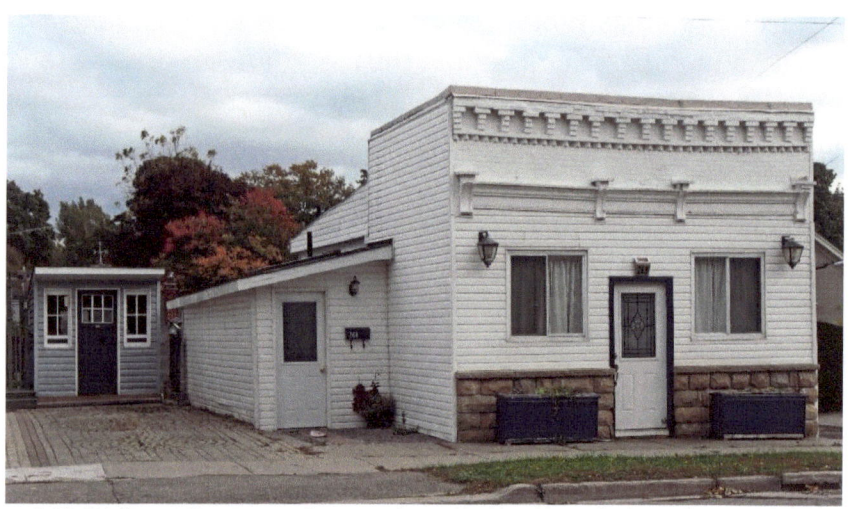

163 Ridout Street – decorative cornice and dentil molding

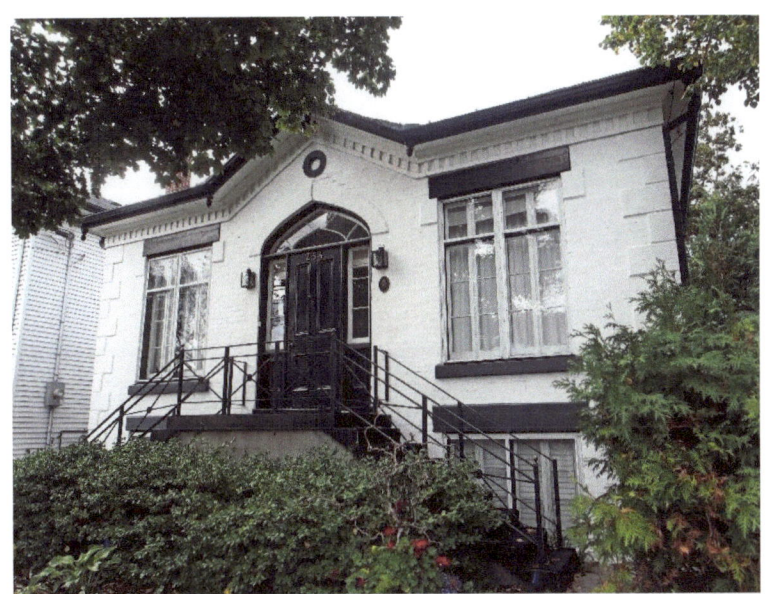

254 Ridout Street – Richard Trick House - c. 1851 - This house is one of the finest examples of a brick Ontario Cottage in Port Hope. It is a raised cottage with the front entrance elevated from street level and approached by double stairs. The heavy lintels of the basement windows form a continuous line with the entrance platform. Capping the house is a low-pitch hipped roof with projecting eaves and a centre gable. The cornice is boxed and has fine crown moulding. Each corner and the ends of the gable have small acorn drops. A turned finial and drop pierce the front gable apex. Beneath the eaves is an interesting brick frieze which consists of protruding brick courses enclosing brick dentilling. An open circle of brickwork decorates the front gable.

All of the front facade windows have timber lintels, which appear to be twice the height of the lugsills below. The main-storey openings hold paired, double-sash windows with doubled, mullioned transoms above. At each window corner, just under the lintels, protruding blocks have been placed. This is a small but classic example of imagination and care on the part of the planner.

The main entrance in its moulded housing consists of a panelled door, flanked by sidelights. Topping the door is an unusual ogee transom with well-arranged muntins. The corners of the house exhibit brick quoins. The entire house is a showcase for the talents of Richard Trick, the original owner of this house, and a prominent local bricklayer.

Richard Trick (1822-1890), originally from Hartland, Devon, England, came to Canada with his brother William about 1836. He established himself as a local mason and was responsible for building many of Port Hope's important brick structures.

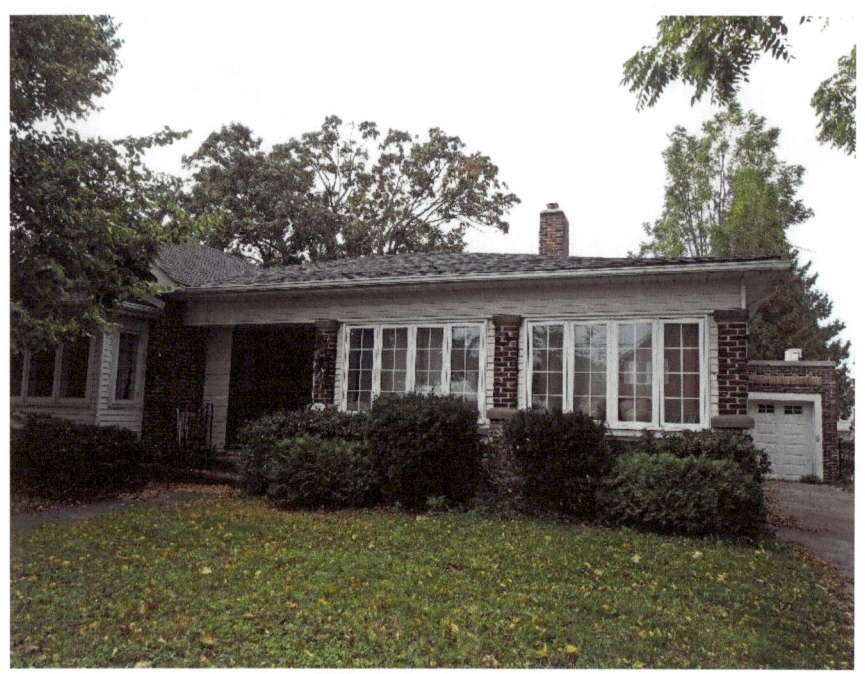

250 Ridout Street

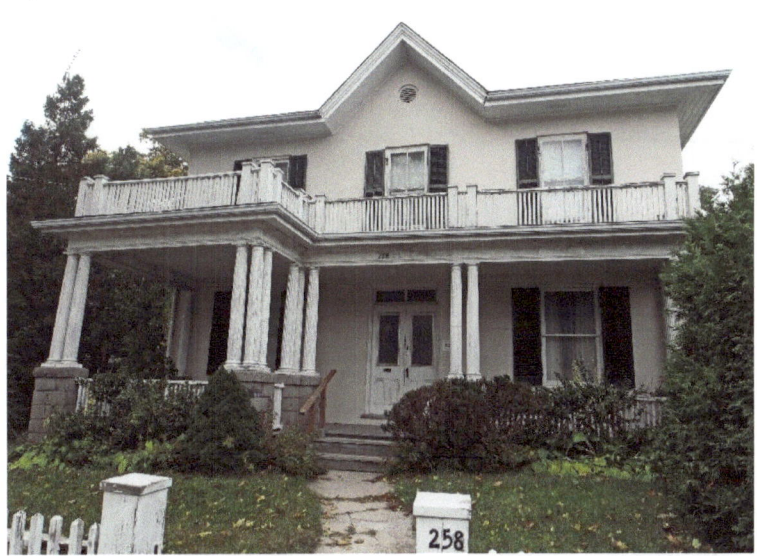

258 Ridout Street - John Lynn House – c. 1857 - This brick house displays a collection of forms from various building styles and cannot be defined as pure style. The gable peak on the main roof line would point to the Ontario Cottage form, and the wide eaves belong to the Greek Revival, while the roof line is Regency. The brick of the house is in the stretcher bond and the house is built on a limestone foundation. The steeply pitched, hipped roof with its centre gable has wide projecting eaves. The cornice is plain and boxed with tongue in groove soffits below. This is a three-bay house, with a centre-hall plan. The large windows are two-over-two and double-hung. They sit on either side of the central opening on both storeys. The second-storey, centre window is narrower, to balance the height and slimness of the main entrance below, and to fit aesthetically into the lines of the gable peak above. All the windows have wooden lugsills below, a soldier course of brick above and horizontally louvred shutters. The circular window in the gable peak, apart from decorating the main facade, allows light into the attic storey of the house.

The main entrance has a set of panelled and windowed doors with a mullioned transom above. The door surround is moulded and the transom recessed. The verandah on the main facade has a flat roof. Its roof railing is comprised of simple, squared spindles with thick, square, tooled posts as supports. Except for the triple posts at the corners, the supports are in pairs. The verandah is deep and is supported by paired columns. At the corners of the verandah, these columns are also tripled. They rest on rusticated block piers. Between the block piers is a handrail supported by squared spindles. The east façade of the house has a two-storey projecting bay that is five sided and capped with a hipped roof. The bay has three windowed sides which all have cast stone lugsills, a soldier course of brick above and leaded glass in the upper portion of the opening.

At the back of the house is a large hipped-roof addition with hipped-roof dormers. It is dressed in clapboard. Another addition at the back is the one-storey sunroom that has leaded glass in the top panes of its windows.

In 1847, Lynn, who was originally from Ireland, was the fire warden for Port Hope. He is best known for building and running the North American Hotel on Walton Street (28-32 Walton Street), which was constructed in 1844. A disastrous fire destroyed the original hotel in the spring of 1850, which burned the structure and its neighbour to the ground. A new building was erected shortly after the fire. By 1857, Mr. Lynn is listed in business directories as a distiller on Cavan Street with the business name of Lynn and White and residing on Ridout Street. In the census of 1861, he provides his age as 57.

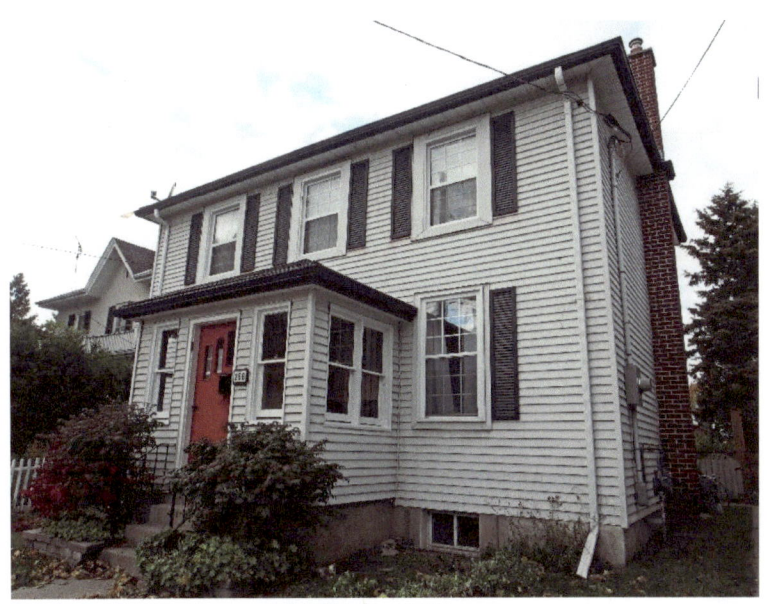

256 Ridout Street

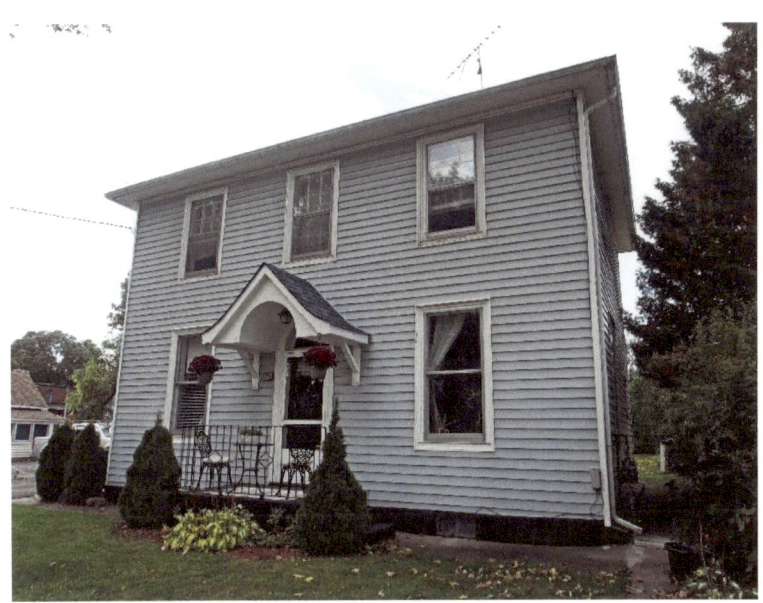

260 Ridout Street

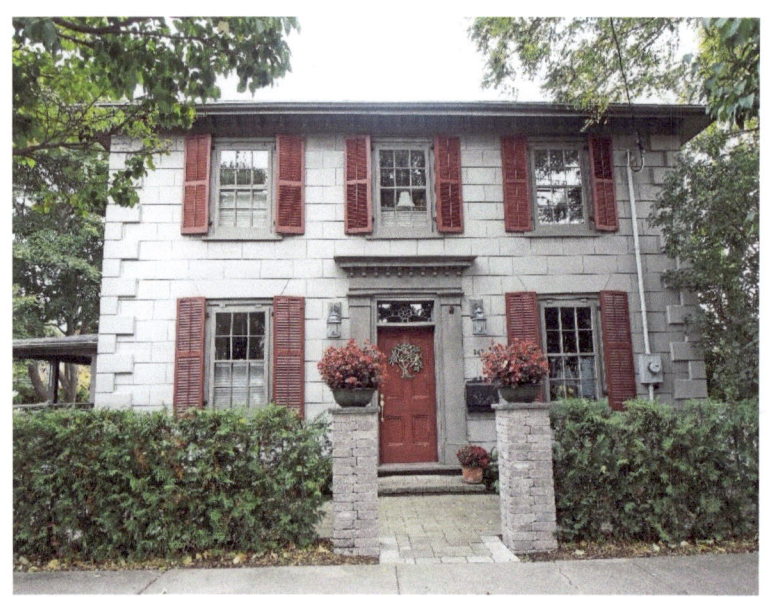

267 Ridout Street – c. 1851 – corner quoins, transom above entrance, multi-paned windows, shutters

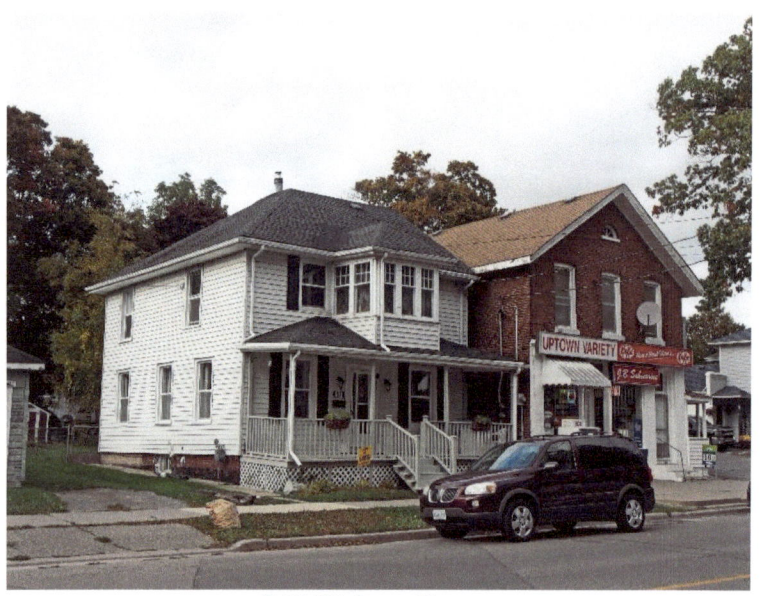

268 Ridout Street

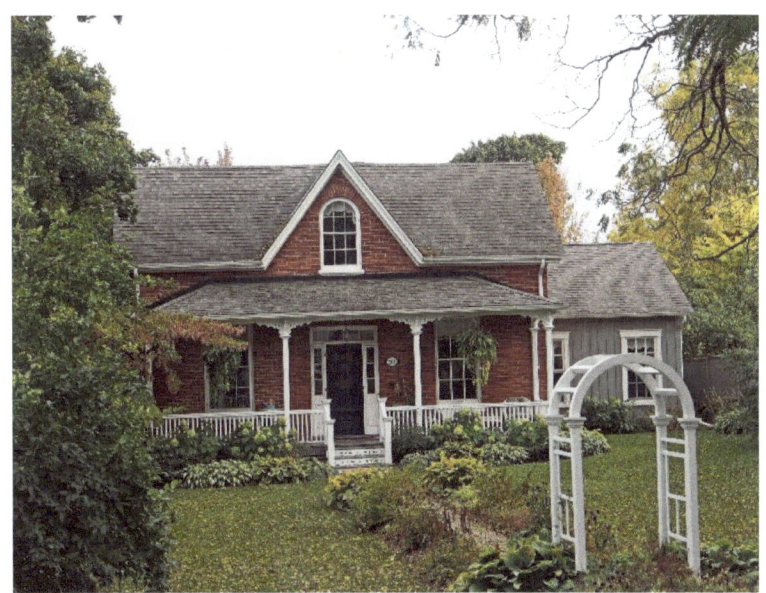

269 Ridout Street – Ontario Cottage

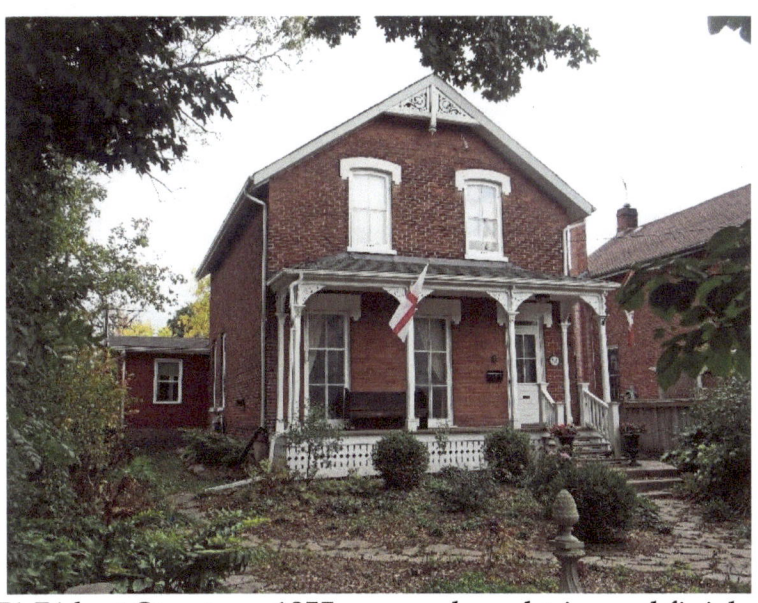

271 Ridout Street – c. 1855 – verge board trim and finial on gable

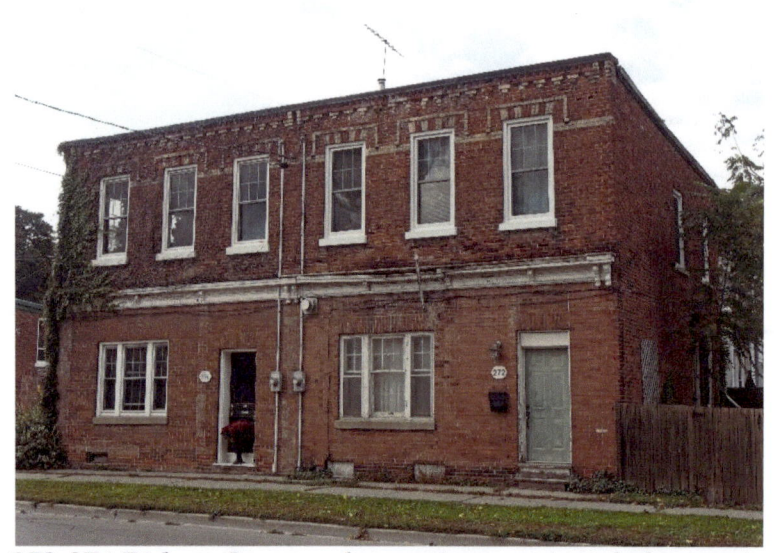

272-274 Ridout Street – decorative cornice, dichromatic voussoirs

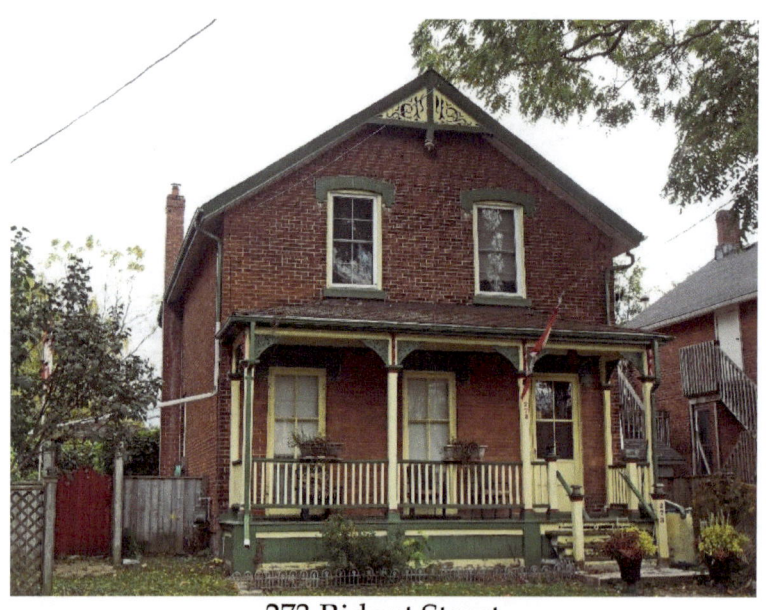

273 Ridout Street

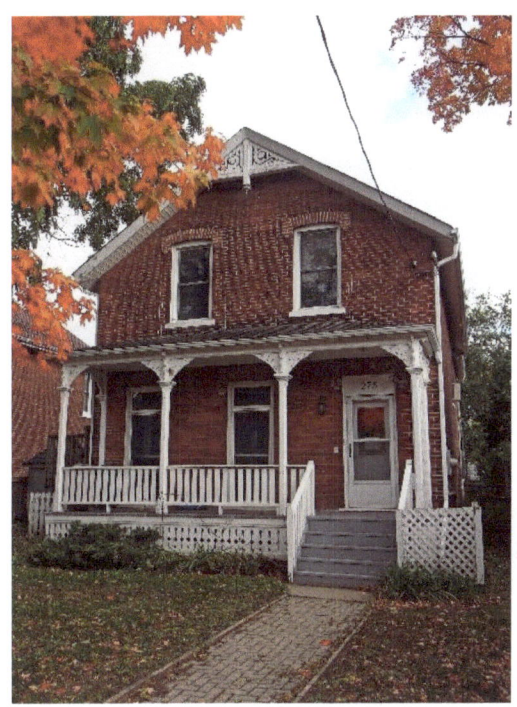

275 Ridout Street

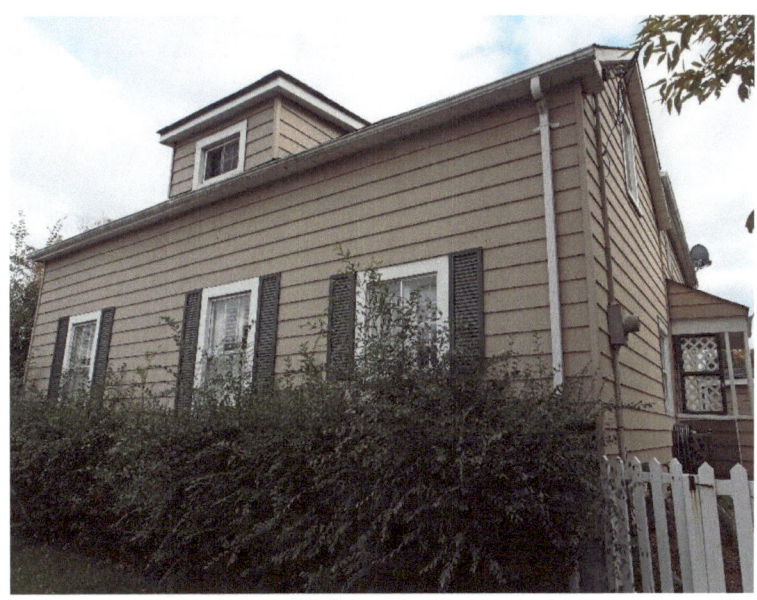

Ridout Street

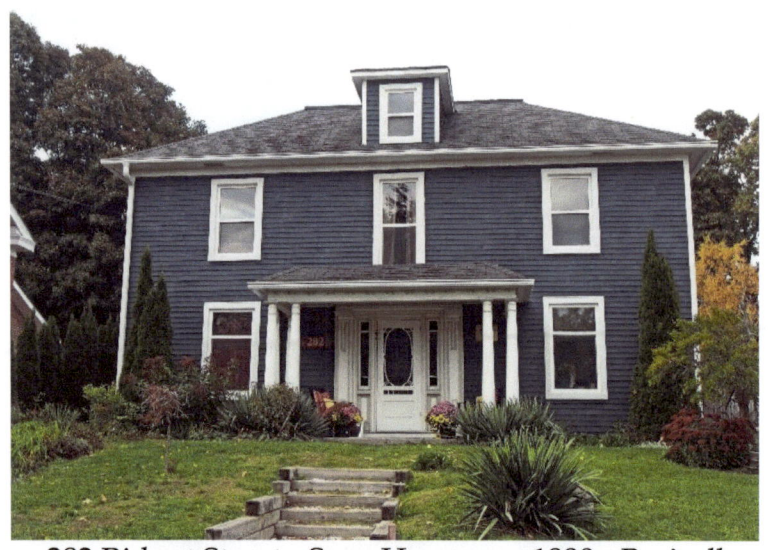

282 Ridout Street - Spry House – c. 1880 - Basically square in plan, this two-storey Neo-Classical frame house is covered in clapboard finished with end boards. Its steeply pitched roof has a flat top section and houses a hipped-roof dormer in the front facade. Together with the projecting eaves are a plain-boxed cornice and an unadorned wooden frieze. The window openings are flat with simple wooden. The first-storey main-facade windows have flat structural openings with a segmental stained-glass pane lying over a flat, clear-glass pane. The centred main door has thin recessed sidelights but no transom panel. The door surround is moulded and emblazoned with an entablature. A columned portico enhances the entrance. The columns are doubled at the front corners and support a flat-topped, hipped roof with boxed cornice and a moulded frieze decorated with tiny, paired dentils.

Thomas Spry (1811-1884), originally from England, was a local blacksmith who had his shop on Cavan Street in the 1850s.

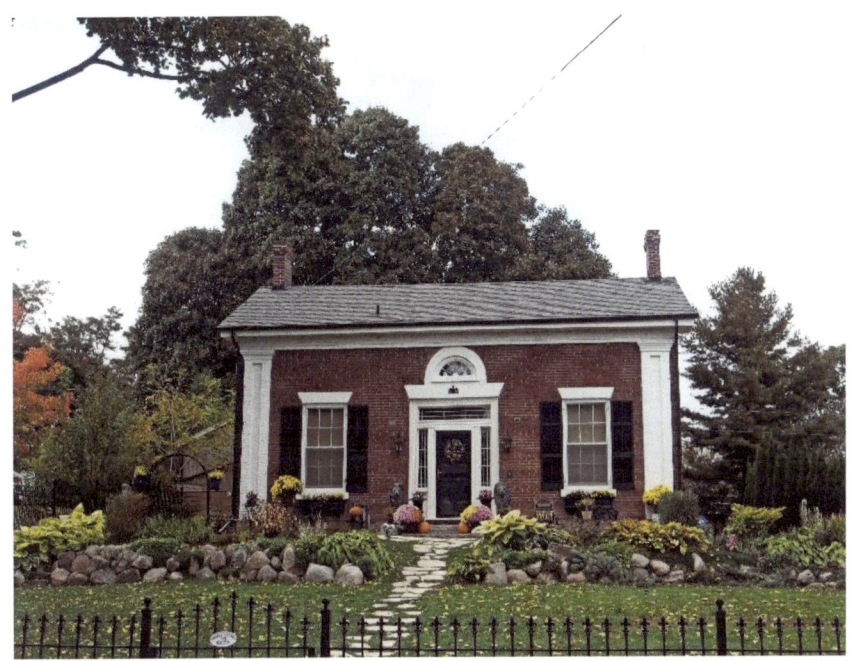

284 Ridout Street - Thomas Spry Cottage (Forge Cottage) – c. 1850 - The house is a good example of local Georgian styling of the one and a half storey cottage design with a centre hall plan, constructed of two course local brick. Some of the features are the brick pilasters, the entrance sidelights and transom. The window above the main door is known as an eyebrow window, which was to provide light to the upstairs hallway.

The large twelve paned windows provide excellent lighting and ventilation most of which is still the original glass. Rectangular multi-paned sidelights and a transom of the same style and dimension flank the Palladian proportioned front entrance. A unique fanlight window that provides light to the upper storey appears to rest on the door lintel.

Forge Cottage was built by Thomas Spry; the name of the cottage is a reference to his trade.

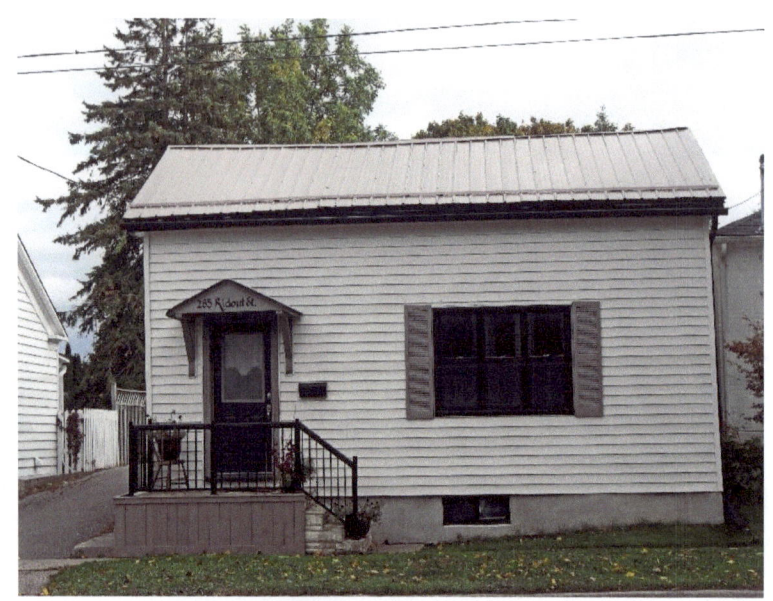
285 Ridout Street

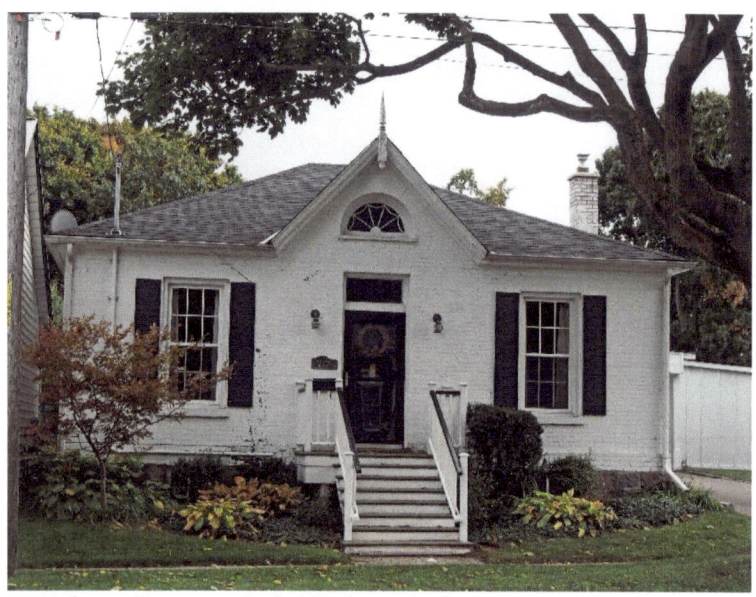
287 Ridout Street - A fanlight window provides light to the upper storey.

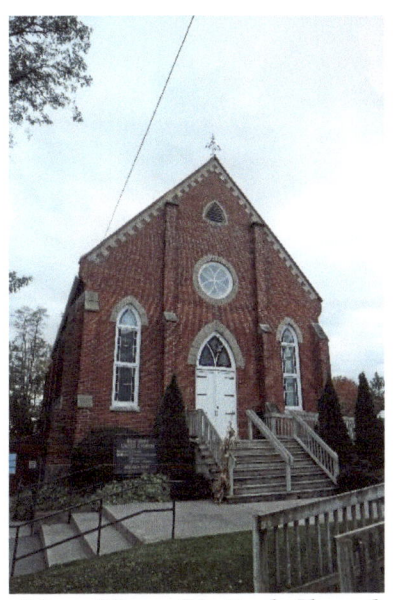

County Road 2 – New Hope United Church – Gothic, lancet
windows, buttresses, dentil molding

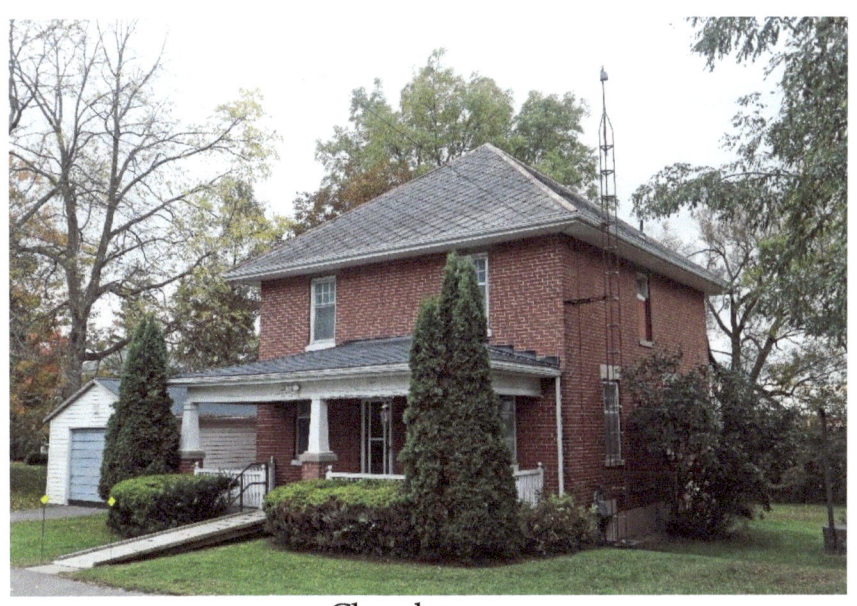

Church manse

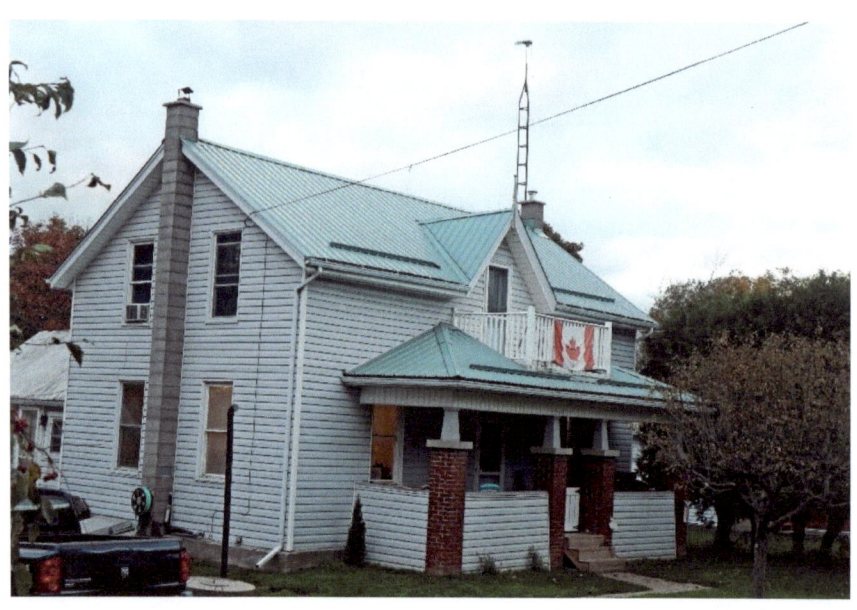

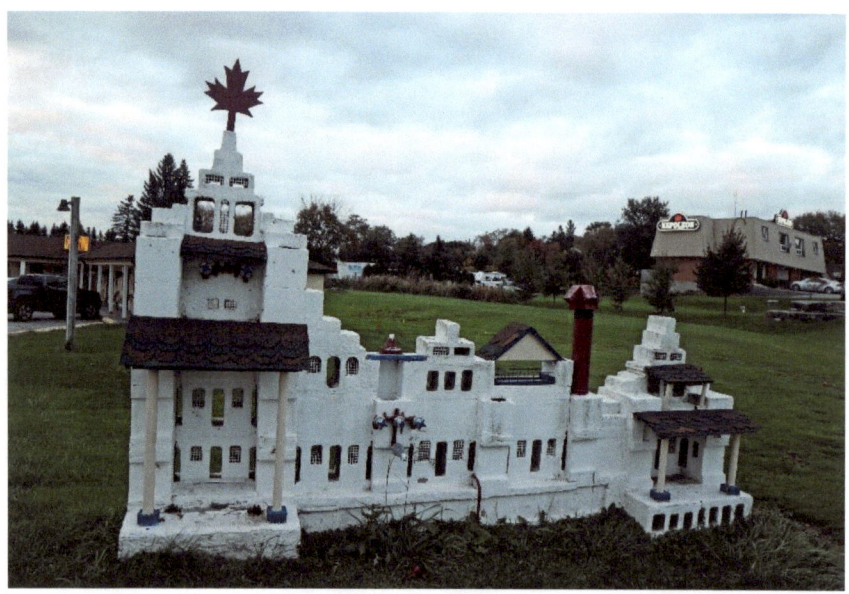

4510 County Road 2 - Budget Inn – at entrance

# Other Books by Barbara Raue

Coins of Gold
Arrows, Indians and Love
The Life and Times of Barbara
The Cromwell Family Book
Laura Secord Discovered
Daddy Where Are You?

Montana Series
Book 1: Montana Dream
Book 2: Life on the Montana Frontier
Book 3: Montana to Boston and Back
Book 4: Montana Sons Go to War
Book 5: Montana Sons Return from War

www.ingramcontent.com/pod-product-compliance
Lightning Source LLC
Chambersburg PA
CBHW041108180526
45172CB00001B/158